POETRY now

AT THE DAWN OF INSPIRATION

Edited by

Sarah Marshall

First published in Great Britain in 2004 by
POETRY NOW
Remus House,
Coltsfoot Drive,
Peterborough, PE2 9JX
Telephone (01733) 898101
Fax (01733) 313524

All Rights Reserved

Copyright Contributors 2004

SB ISBN 1 84460 843 3

FOREWORD

Although we are a nation of poets we are accused of not reading poetry, or buying poetry books. After many years of listening to the incessant gripes of poetry publishers, I can only assume that the books they publish, in general, are books that most people do not want to read.

Poetry should not be obscure, introverted, and as cryptic as a crossword puzzle: it is the poet's duty to reach out and embrace the world.

The world owes the poet nothing and we should not be expected to dig and delve into a rambling discourse searching for some inner meaning.

The reason we write poetry (and almost all of us do) is because we want to communicate: an ideal; an idea; or a specific feeling. Poetry is as essential in communication, as a letter; a radio; a telephone, and the main criterion for selecting the poems in this anthology is very simple: they communicate.

CONTENTS

Lost Love	Janet Pocock	1
A Beggar Boy's Riches	Dennis Corkin	2
Future Life	Steve West	3
Prayer Of Innocence	Kevin Eccleston	4
The Rookie Bowler's Lament	Richard Foster	5
Marooned	R Ellis	6
Seasons	Gillian Walters	7
Man's Best Friend	Clive Hughes	8
The Shed	NJH	9
Breathe Again	I J Penn	10
Strange Thoughts	B M Butler	11
Love	Jonathan Gilbert	12
My Cat Timothy Darious	M Haswell	13
My Life	Alex C Neill	14
For Mum	Lynn Trunley Smith	15
My Secret	Mimie	16
Video Queen	Michelle Bennett	17
Willpower	Stuart Levett	18
Pirates	John Rafferty	19
The Magnolia Tree	Jeanne Hoare-Matthews	20
Golden Memories	Elaine Henley	21
Across The Sea	Pete Robins	22
What Does It Take?	Sarah Shovlin	23
XX/XY	A Harvey	24
The Naturist	Ray Smith	25
Broken Doll	D Unwin	26
Farewell, Slam Doors	David Spanton	27
Spooky Night	Michaela Baldwin	28
Megan	Tuesday Hawkes	29
Our Baby Girl	K Succamore	30
What Makes Me Cry?	Kevin Stuart Robison	31
Dreamland	Harpreet K Bhelley	32
Stalker	Ian McNamara	33
The Seasons	F Elliott	34
Lost For Words?	Errol A Johnson	35
Burnt-Out Shell	Geoff Beatty	36

Through The Eyes Of A Child	Kathleen Christine Bennett	37
One Set Shy, The Other Mocking	Anne Logan	38
Photo Booth	V A Coulson	39
Blinded	Lee Connor	40
If	Graham Connor	41
St Valentine's Day	Charles Hardman	42
Sights Of Spring	Maureen Reeves	43
Letter For The Future	Violet Cowley	44
An Ode To Marty	Marie Gallagher	45
Whenever People Look At Me . . .	Lauren Allinson	46
The Farm	Alan Tucker	47
Untitled	D M Strange	48
My Grandson - Ethan Beard	Terry Rowberry	49
The Beauty Of God's Love	V P Lovell	50
Remember	Jean Turner	51
Love Or Possession?	Al Môn	52
Spring	P McIlquham	53
The Perfect Friend	Eleanor Knipe	54
I Love Him All The Same	Zoë Margo Pearce	55
The Sounds Of The Sea	T Smithies	56
Weather Forecast	Brian Parvin	57
Against Terror	Steven J Smith	58
The Four Year Old	John Charles Porter	60
Going Home	D Streek	61
An Ode To A Memory	Sidney Dudson	62
The Wrath Of Mankind	S Tranter	64
Searching For Magic	Mathew Watkins	65
The Fall	Walter Sinclair	66
Free	Maria Riccardi	67
My Beloved	G Bryant	68
The Miracle Of David	Mary Plumb	69
Drought	Louis Foley	70
A Vitriolic Romance	Elaine Borowski	71
Spring	Sue Byham	72
Mummy	Emma Lockyer	73
The Gardener's Lot	Yvonne Bulman Peters	74
By Moonlight	Wendy Simpson	75
The Symbolic Tree	Muriel Billyard Bond	76

A Message For Dad	Amanda Stredwick	77
The Fishermen	T J Styles	78
The Reality Of War	Amanda Jayne Hibbert	79
The Visitor	Len Mann	80
The Loss Of A Loved One	Myria Hayers	81
Fill That Space	D Ierotheou	82
World Of Peace	G Breakspear	83
A World Gone Mad	R A Hinson	84
Just Think About It	Dai Jon Maddocks	86
Love Never Dies	Karl Wade	87
Our Albert's A VIP	Brian Denton	88
Growing Up	Jean Yates	90
Poor Old Soul	Brian M Wood	91
Terrorists Strike Again	Rosemary Davies	92
You There	John El Wright	93
Like Saint Peter, Learning	Peter Asher	94
Vegetarians Versus Meat Eaters	Keith Jackson	95
Storms	Jean Donne	96
Whisper Inside A Broken Child	Jasmyn Galley	97
Colours	Tim Johnson	98
Who Is God?	K R Kadkol	99
The Street With No Name	Jocelyne Trickett	100
The Monument	William Birtwistle	101
Our Multicultural World	Jane Limani	102
What Do You Do?	D E Hampshire	103
Fate Is Great	Darren Protheroe	104
Screaming Friends' Pursuit	Marie Jones	105
Live Life	Jeanette Styles	106
In The End	Johannes Robert McCormack	107
The Fields Of Tibet	D Johnson	108
The Cook	G Andrews	109
A Chicken To Pluck	Donata Richards	110
What You Are To Me	Margaret Waudby	112
Christmas In The Village	Kevin Kondol	113
Housewife's Revenge	Lesley Paul	114
The Cat	May Elliston	115
Our School	D M Higgins	116
My Beloved	Anon	117

Think Of Me	Pam Burley	118
England 2004	Pamela Rossiter	119
Where Love So Tainted Dwells	Ryan Kelly	120
The Lovebirds	R Thompson	121
Why?	Becky Joyce	122
Because I Love You	Lynda Carol Beardmore	123
Devil's Dust	Steven Wilson	124
There's A Love	Beth	125
I Won't Believe	T Milner	126
An Eternal Relationship	Marco Nigro	127
Babysitting Blues	Kathy Duncan	128
Eve Of Love	Martin Bevan	129
Mongrels	D Mullings-Powell	130
Rite Of Passage	Fay Smith	132
So Tired	Sheena Harris	133
Love Is Eternal	Emmanuel Petrakis	134
Roundabout Of Life	Sheila Walters	135
My Grandma	Gill Green	136
The Days Of The West Are Dead	Edward Mathieson	137
Busy Hands	Pauline Bunkin	138
Full Circle	Avril Brown	139
My Black Rose	Roy Jackson	140
A Beautiful Mind	S Beverly-Ruff	141
Untitled	Fran Gardner	142
My Twilight World	Robert Beach	144
I Wish	Rachel Krastins	145
Looking Back From Above	Michael Chambers	146
Intoxicated Demons	Mathew Cullum	147
The Gardening Club	Edith Mary Wilson	148
Altars	James Knox Whittet	149
Dragon Tales - Timothy Thomas	Olive R Thomson	150
Troubled Mind	Alexander Campbell	151
CJ	James Gallagher	152
Raindrop	Alan Brafield	154

LOST LOVE

I wanted to send you a card,
But I thought it would be too hard.
It's our anniversary today and you don't seem to care,
All I can feel is great despair.

I look at you and feel so sad,
And wonder what I did that was so bad.
Lovely home, lovely kids, holidays galore,
All this we are to have no more.

I can't believe that this is the end,
It's really driving me round the bend.
Getting older is no joke,
But I don't want another bloke.

I feel so lonely on my own,
Boys grown up, always on the phone.
What a shame we can't talk,
We always could, at least I thought.

We made our vows a long time ago,
I didn't think we'd come to blows,
Happy anniversary is what I want to say,
From me to you this very day.

Janet Pocock

A Beggar Boy's Riches

A beggar boy is what I am
No home, no clothes, or money
People stop and stare at me
To them I may look funny.

I'm dressed in clothes all tattered and torn
My shoes the same, right through they're worn
But really I'm rich, as rich as can be
What God gave to nature, he also gave me.

He gave me the Earth, that I may lie down
And share with the flowers, a bed on the ground
He gave me the stars that light up the night
A picturesque scene, and a beautiful sight.

From the trees, I get fruit that I feed on
From the streams I get water to drink,
And when I am full, I have reason
To lay down and have a good sleep.

So the next time you happen to see me
Don't think, I'm unhappy, and sad
For these riches, from nature, have made me
Happy, contented and glad.

Dennis Corkin

FUTURE LIFE

Punch drunk after many rounds
This fox will still outstrip the hounds.
Depressing feelings sights and sounds
My past sad life's now out of bounds.

This lonely illness fuelled my fears
It took so many younger years.
The pain and turmoil no one hears.
Be gone forever - no more tears.

Steve West

PRAYER OF INNOCENCE

Power and might with God on his side
He just kept on although I cried
For him to stop my childhood pain
I tried and tried I tried in vain
To be at one with hopes and dreams
Of childlike things but no one seems
To know the terror felt inside
Power and might and God on his side.

He is so right and I'm so wrong
And no one hears the children's song
Of innocence and desperate prayer
Does no one hear or give a care
To rescue me from evil's grasp
To make this night the very last
I shall endure the hurt and fear
Of blessed Reverend Father dear.

So just keep quiet and just be good
Like all good Catholic children should
Don't tell the evil this man does
Because his God is watching us
That's what our teacher said in class
And what the Devil said at mass
I still remember to this day
To rot in Hell his soul I pray

So when you hear your children cry
And see the glint in Father's eye
Don't dare ignore the warning signs
Or cover up these awful crimes
That he commits with evil lust
Speak out speak out you know you must
Stand up stand up with adult pride
With power and might and God on your side.

Kevin Eccleston

THE ROOKIE BOWLER'S LAMENT

I know I am a rookie
and haven't got the knack,
of how you have to roll the bowl
to land beside the jack.

There are others round about me
who used to be the same,
and only with lots of practice
became experts in their game.

I really feel a dodo
when I land inside the ditch,
or when I get the bias wrong
and land in someone's pitch.

I used to wonder what they meant
when they shouted, 'Take more grass!'
They forgot that I am human
and not a silly ass.

Someday I'll learn to roll it right
and help to win the tie.
I hope it doesn't take too long
and that day will soon be nigh.

So come away you rookies,
you don't have to take the blame.
You're only just a learner,
and it's only just a game!

Richard Foster

MAROONED

How long have I been here,
Not daring to take one step forward,
Nor one step back?
The heat and smells are making me dizzy
But I must *not* move.
Harsh, discordant sounds and a
Kaleidoscope of colours surround me.
How long can I last?
Must take stock of my possessions,
Three cigarettes and lighter,
One small loaf,
One packet of biscuits,
Small carton of milk,
Wish I had brought that lemonade now,
Throat is so dry.
Won't be missed yet, not until teatime at least.
Oh how long can I last out?
Can feel myself swaying.
Suddenly, the sounds hush,
The colours stop flashing by.
I can move.
One car has stopped.
The motorist raises a friendly finger.
I step down from the traffic island
And cross the few feet to safety.

R Ellis

SEASONS

Spring is bursting full of life,
When buds burst through, bringing crocus,
Yellow and blue.

Each day grows longer,
Spring flowers stronger,
Some meadows a carpet of colour.

The birds are busy, it's time to nest,
Onward now there'll be no rest,
Twigs and moss with mud to pack,
A perfect home for a brood to hatch.

Spring is such a lovely season,
Which gives us all that one good reason,
For all us humans, friend or foe.

To help each other as we go
Along the path that we've been given,
To help to make life worth living.

Gillian Walters

Man's Best Friend

Always excited like not seen me before
My dog wags its tail and waits at the door.
Greeting me, jumping up with a lick
At my feet drops a ball for me to kick.

Glee in eyes, floppy ears they curl
Jumping and playing, head's in a whirl.
Lies by my side for rest and for fuss
Showing me affection, so full of trust.

At bedtime follows to see what's new
Lying at my feet, my dog sticks like glue.
Quiet and content the peace they share,
Tell you all folks, sure beats a bear.

At morning wakes me up wagging its tail
Barks at the postman delivering the mail.
My dog I love and cherish too
Friends like this are far and few.

Clive Hughes

THE SHED

As Colin, John and me, we're taking apart a shed,
The wind was really blowing, swirling around our heads.
We had taken down the sides, and about to remove the top
When a mighty gust of wind blew up and went and caught the lot.
It flew into the air and came crashing to the ground
And broke into a million pieces spreading all around,
Well I looked over at John and he looked over at Colin,
And he just cracked up laughing and we were soon following.
Tears were filling up our eyes, our stomachs ached like mad,
Yet why were we so happy, when what we'd done was bad?
Eventually we stopped laughing, thinking of an excuse
Of what we could tell Ken on how we'd smashed his roof.
So after getting our act together, we told the truth instead,
And now, up to this very day, I'll never forget that shed.

NJH

BREATHE AGAIN

Gaze your thoughts to views of far
Where horizons clash against the stars
The time of day could slip you by
As you lie back, with the clouds you fly
You glide above a gentle sea
And watch your dreams swim so free
You reach to touch and grasp this scene
Your fingers brush against your dreams
A rush of magic through your hands
That lifts you higher from the sands
The sands of time that try to slow
Your lifetime flight, with the wind you flow
A land of tears approaches near
You fly above and past your fear
'Cause now you're aiming for the sun
The warmth, the light that drives your fun
The love, the joy that holds your heart
Miles from here your flight did start
And you by now are strong and bold
You took your life from the winter cold
You broke the ice and flew so free
And now can see what you wish to be
There are no more fears and no more pain
For once, you learn to breathe again.

I J Penn

STRANGE THOUGHTS

I'm sitting here and thinking
Of the times I've spent with you
Alone in this old armchair
That's got room enough for two.

We used to sit here often
Now the chair seems big and bare,
Yet I sit here thinking
Of the lovely times we share.

I sometimes cry myself to sleep
But your memories will not die,
I know I must forget you know
But this chair won't let me try.

It was just over a year ago
I can't control the pain
The chair seems to tell me
That I'll never feel the same.

B M Butler

Love

Love will always be a million miles away from me.
As I look up to the stars I see the things that should be.
I wish you were with me, but for me
Love will always be a sleeping dream.
Memories blow through my lonely heart.
Within a twinkle of a star I am in your world of dreams,
Your love for me is like a whispered flame,
There is no time in love,
Never shall it be when love is with me
And as the echoes of darkness surround me
I know that your name will forever be
Written in my darkest shadow for all eternity.

Jonathan Gilbert

MY CAT TIMOTHY DARIOUS

My cat is grey
He's big and fat
Loves to eat breakfast
Stretches out on the mat
Sleeps all day
When he wakes up he likes to play.

He loves sitting on the chair
Looks out of the window
When no one's around
Opens the doors without a sound.

Creeps upstairs
Wakes us up out of bed
With a loud miaow
As much as to say
Where's my breakfast
I haven't been fed.

I tell him my troubles
He's very wise
I always listen
To his good advice
Well he says miaow
In his pussy cat way
So I know he listens
To what I say.

I love him
And he loves me
Best friends forever
We will be, Timothy Darious and me.

M Haswell

My Life

At just past sixty years of age
What do I write on this page?
Memories of the village school
Where the teacher we had was nobody's fool,
A move to Edinburgh we made,
Where in different parts we stayed,
But back at holiday time we would go
To see relations and friends that we did know.
I've travelled around a bit since then
After leaving Edinburgh aged three times ten.
Redundancy has twice been a part of my life,
The first time it happened I met my wife,
But now in Witney we are a family of four,
Who knows what the future has in store?

Alex C Neill

FOR MUM

The love of a mother
Is like the warmth from the sun
It shines like no other
From the day you were born
With mother and child
The bond is unbroken
With miles in between
And words left unspoken
My mother's my home
Wherever she be
My heart lives in her
And her heart lives in me
Our love is forever
It's deep and it's true
I will always be grateful
For a mother like you

I love you.

Lynn Trunley Smith

My Secret

I wake in the morning, then dress and start my day,
I sit and have my breakfast and then I'm away,
to my job as a teacher in a primary school,
where the children and I have to work to rule!

I look the same, I speak the same, but I have an inner glow,
and those that know me well enough say I let it show,
in the way I laugh and the sparkle in my eyes,
and the reason I am like this has taken me by surprise.

I wait each day for night to come and in the darkness of my room,
I turn on my computer and know that now quite soon,
I'll see your name up on the screen and we are alone once more,
to share our thoughts, our highs and lows like we have never done before.

We are M'Lord and Lady, a game we like to play,
we've never met and yet I know that you are here to stay.
It's a kind of magic, unreal and yet so true,
this secret part of my life that I only share with you.

Mimie

VIDEO QUEEN

I have a very special friend
Who likes to watch TV,
She stars up all the programmes
That she cannot wait to see.

She likes to be quite organised
Puts her choices into charts,
But when the programmes start to clash,
That's when the real fun starts.

She has to set her videos,
There's one in every room
And when she's used all her machines
Down the street she'll zoom.

She'll ask the next door neighbour
And the man across the street,
The milkman and the postie,
She won't admit defeat.

With all her programmes covered,
There's nothing more to do
But head back home, pull up a chair
There's last week's videos to view!

Michelle Bennett

WILLPOWER

When I got home from work today
I saw - in the kitchen - to my dismay
A tray of cakes and some mince pies
A feast of goodies beheld my eyes
I looked around in deep despair
My tummy said, 'Shall I prepare?'
I said, 'Oh Lord - what shall I do?'
With these mince pies and choc cake too
If I start now - I'll never stop
At least until the buttons pop

So help me please - make up my mind
To make these cakes was very kind
But spare a thought for my poor figure
If I eat this lot I'll get much bigger.
I will have to look - then turn away
Resist temptation - come what may
Don't eat these cakes you foolish man
They'll make you fat - it's part of the plan

But then I think - she's worked quite hard
With currants, flour and lumps of lard
To make these cakes that smell so nice
With creamy fillings and tops of ice
I suppose I'd best not spoil her fun
What the hell - I'll try just one.

Stuart Levett

PIRATES

Out of Hell's Kitchen, far from Hell Gill,
the dance of the skull and crossbones
ripples in the curve of Hell's Mouth.

Here the daredevils lie in wait,
under the loom of Snowdonia,
to intercept and beard the unwary,

the reckless form the lost vessels
of each armada. You can see the whole
of Cardigan Bay from the summit

but cannot pronounce Pwllheli,
nor disperse the marauding family
kicking sandcastles into the air,

unleashing all manner of demons
to challenge the faith of Saint Tudwal
and terrify the solitary nun,

two wardens and four hundred sheep
of Bardsey Island. Over the side
with the cabin boy, who resurfaces

to report a litter of bronze cannon,
half-buried and encrusted, and shot
nearby, like dung in regular heaps.

To the sound of a mariner keelhauled
and shrieking gull thievery, it's away
past the jaws of Skomer and Skokholm

to the Channel and the Atlantic,
where there are reputations and prices
on heads, and forever grinning dolphins.

John Rafferty

THE MAGNOLIA TREE

How beautiful your magnolia tree looks
bathing in the incandescent moonlight!
Her delicately sculptured flowers
each one cupped like a catholic candle
as if each was emblazoned as a
friend we have known - now long gone.
See how her silvery shadows conciliate
with her pink-lipped buds and sturdy stem,
see how she curtseys adieu as we homeward pass
stirred by the fragrant freshening breeze,
and our wine-warmed mouths whisper
their own fond familiar farewells.

Jeanne Hoare-Matthews

GOLDEN MEMORIES

His step is so slow, his back is bent
He walks now with a stick, his days are spent
Remember old times with friends so few
Of boyhood days that he once knew

A face that is worn with cares of life
Softens with a tear remembering his wife
The face that time cannot erase
Calls him now from another age

Golden memories cherished and rare
Are all that's left in a lonely stare
Life's toils and troubles have ebbed and flowed
Soften with laughter and blessing bestowed

When life was at a gentler pace
Time was slower not in a race
Contented again in dreams of the past
Regretting sometimes that they cannot last

Amazed how quickly the days drift by
And knowing that some time he must fly
Back to the past where loved ones await
Hoping that he is not too late

Again in his arms his love so fair
Together they will climb the golden stair

A friendly touch, a helping hand
Steadying him as he tries to stand

Walking life's path for a little time more
Wondering what life has yet in store.

Elaine Henley

Across The Sea

It's a cold, wet day, as I stand here alone,
Gazing out, far across the sea,
I feel so alone, my heart feeling like a stone,
Because you are not here with me.

The rain lashes down,
The wind whips my face,
As I gaze out over the sea,
I need to hold you today, but you're so far away,
Oh Lord, tell me, why must this be?

My arms are aching to hold you,
My hands are longing to touch
Your smiling face, you're my one special girl,
You're the one that I love so much.

From across the sea, you've stolen my heart,
You make me feel like no other could,
From the very first time I met you, my love,
I knew that someday, you would.

You're the reason I wake up at dawn every day,
And go and stand alone by the sea,
I could stand there all day, as time passes away,
Just wishing you were here with me.

From across the sea,
My heart's calling your name,
It whispers, 'Darling, it won't be long now,
We'll be together real soon, my darling, I swear,
Be strong, we'll make it somehow.'

Pete Robins

WHAT DOES IT TAKE?

I woke up this morning, as happy as could be
For there in the paper was a message for me
All poets wanted, so send in your prose
With these words in my head, I immediately arose

I sought out my pen and then started to write
But the words wouldn't come, as try as I might
I wrote this and that, but nothing would rhyme
I've reached the conclusion that I've wasted my time.

But as I'm a trier, I just battled on
But sadly for me, the words had all gone
My poor brain was tired, it had need of a rest
I just couldn't blame it, it had been put to the test.

So I put down my pen, went out for some air
Refreshed and revived, I resumed with great care
But just as before, nothing came to my mind
I had to acknowledge that my brain had declined.

I just have to accept that I'm not really a poet
Because if I were, I would be able to show it
But I'd just like to know, that as I'm a beginner
Please what does it take to make me a winner?

Sarah Shovlin

XX/XY

People dancing lost in sound
Kiss your neck turn you round
I touch you now feeling bolder
Hold you close kiss your shoulder

I run my hand along your thighs
You turn to face me big brown eyes
Pull you close hands on hips
Bending close brush your lips

You take my hand we leave that floor
Pushing through the toilet door
Against the wall I need a taste
Lift your legs around my waist

Feel the music in your chest
Feel the brush of flesh on flesh
Feel it pumping through your veins
Feel the chemicals in my brain

Morning and I'm feeling ill
S**t, were you on the pill?
Unused condoms, vomit stains
Now you're gone, what's your name?

A Harvey

THE NATURIST

No clothes to cling to your skin
No pockets to put your money in
Things like this will be missed
If you become a naturist

No bra to support your breast
Hanging loose like all the rest
Men standing there, naked with pride
And their manhood dangling from side to side

Being a naturist is not always good fun
Like walking bare in the hot daytime sun
It has its dangers mind you
Be careful when you have a barbecue

Get too close and the fat might spit
And land on your tender bit

Ray Smith

Broken Doll

Beware, dearest daughter, beware of the silent ones,
For now they are all but whispers tendered within the edifice of time.
Beware, dearest daughter,
For they are far less merciful . . . than I.

Even in death, my spirit cries out to her,
Weeping for the youth that was raped . . . the innocence that
                                            was defiled . . .
Her pale, childlike, porcelain face
Now shattered into a thousand tiny fragments
Of lifeless beauty . . . each reflecting its own
I laugh at the mockery and irony of fate . . .
For she spares no one as she dances hand in hand with time.
She taunts us with her invisible smile,
A smile which to me reflects only a masque,
A mask which my face can no longer wear
Do you remember
Fingers of sunlight
As they were caressing your face?
Do you remember
The leaves dancing in the sky,
Then falling softly to their painless death?
And they are always asking me
Why must we forgive . . .
If only to forgive, if never to forget . . .
Read these words which are engraved upon my face
And then look away . . . look away . . .

D Unwin

FAREWELL, SLAM DOORS

They glide shut oh so smoothly,
The doors on the latest trains,
Don't hang, half open, loosely,
Hurrah for the modern brains!

They don't provide the wake up,
The entry to today's cause,
Make one jump, like startled pup,
To the noise of slamming doors.

It's a greater start to work,
That, no one can now refute,
With less tendency to shirk,
If your fate is to commute.

The walk along's more pleasant,
From the station to workplace,
Good things of life, incessant,
'Stead of a nerve-jangling haste.

One thing to all is certain,
Now, the gentle sound of waves,
Can ease our daily burden,
As we all become wage slaves.

For there's less chance of a headache,
To begin the working day,
Thanks due then, to those who take
The noise of 'slam doors' away!

David Spanton

SPOOKY NIGHT

The night is so dark, the night is so cold,
Up on the spooky hill the house has been sold
Whoever goes in, doesn't come out
There must be some kind of a spook about.

It's half-past twelve in the middle of the night
The family arrives in for a fight.
They went into the lounge and there they see
A ghost that looks just like me.

I was only sitting in a rocking chair
And then they began to stare,
Then they ran and started to yell and scream,
I went, 'Don't be so mean.'

After, when the family was back out
Mark said, 'I knew there was a spook about.'
But will the spook come back again?
I don't think so, I saw it catch a train.

The ghost has gone, gone for good
The house just lays there in the mud
What if it came back to this place?
Oh that would be really ace.

Michaela Baldwin (11)

MEGAN

I'm only a few weeks old baby,
And yet I'm so alert.
The adults all think I'm clever,
And not a little squirt.

My mum is Lindsey McClure
And my dad is Nicky Hawkes.
The adults all think I'm clever,
I'll be the baby that talks.

My skin is so soft and peachy,
Am I really that lovely?
The adults all think I'm clever,
I'm born, so open the bubbly.

My birthday is February eighth,
I was born a leader,
The adults all think I'm clever,
My name is Megan Alida!

Tuesday Hawkes (13)

Our Baby Girl

Little Lorna, our baby girl
Has bright blue eyes and a sausage curl.
Cherry lips and enchanting smile
She makes our world seem so worthwhile.
Little arms reach out for me
I take her hands so tenderly,
Her lovely smile breaks forth like sun,
Embracing each and everyone.
I hold her close so soft and dear
To keep her safe from harm and fear.
Then she turns to her daddy, as if to say,
'Take me for I love you today.'
She snuggles her head up to his face,
Not minding his harsh chin,
The little arms go around his neck
As though she's loving him.
Although I feed her, and keep her clean,
Shiny as a pearl,
And I know she loves me very much,
She's still her daddy's girl,
Little bright eyes full of fun,
Full of mischief too,
Our happiness is now complete,
For baby we have you.
Your mummy and daddy are so in love,
And as happy as we can be,
Before you came there was just us two,
God blessed us and made us three.

K Succamore

WHAT MAKES ME CRY?

What is the point in life if you are all alone?
What is the point in love when your heart feels like a stone?
What is the point in air when you no longer want to breathe?
What is the point in a door when you can no longer leave?
What is the point in friends when they no longer call you?
What is the point in speech when there is no one left to talk to?
What is the point in sight when all you see is black?
What is the point in reaching out when you know they'll never look back?
What is the point of it all, I sit and ask myself why?
I guess no one will ever know and that's what makes me cry.

Kevin Stuart Robison

DREAMLAND

Above the clouds,
Where birds don't even reach,
I sit upon the silken clouds,
Where I sleep.

Where night never falls,
And day never goes,
A place of eternal beauty,
By the silent falls.

The soft wings that you grow,
And your halo that forms,
And the animals
Bounce around.

Where dreams will come true,
Anything you dream to do,
Your dreams will come true,
Anything in the world,
That you dream to do . . .

Harpreet K Bhelley (11)

STALKER

I am a fighter, killer and thief,
The greatest man ever to have sinned!
Tortured like a slave, even though I am a chief,
I am the trees, I am the wind,
I am the one who disappoints, the one who upsets,
A dreamer awakened at last,
I am just another man who deserves what he gets,
I am the future, I am the past,
I am the wrong example preached from the pulpit,
The prompting persuader before they commence,
In every bad situation I am the culprit!
I am the local pervert sitting on your fence,
I am why your dog barks every night!
An inflicter who has battered and bruised,
I am a whistling shadow under the streetlight,
I am the troublemaker, I am the accused,
I am a spirit in your house that nobody can budge,
The most pleasing name on the witness's report,
A serial rapist before the judge,
I am your host for the evening, in the dock of the court.

Ian McNamara

THE SEASONS

I woke one morning to hear the birds sing
And welcome in another spring
As the days went by I walked up the dene
Where all the leaves were turning green

Then I stood and looked up high
And watched the swallows in the sky
It really filled my heart with cheer
To know that summertime was here

As I stand in the sun's warm glow
That makes the grass and flowers grow
I turn around and give a sigh
At clouds appearing in the sky

As time goes by the weather grows cold
Changing the leaves to yellow and gold
So I walk again, back thro' the dene
And there survey the autumn scene

The leaves are falling all around
Making a carpet on the ground
And as I sit by the fire's glow
I look thro' the window and see the first snow

The days of winter go slowly by
The snow keeps falling from the sky
As I stand and look, I'm sure of one thing
I'll wake one morning and hear the birds sing

To herald in another spring

F Elliott

LOST FOR WORDS?

Someone wants me to compile a poem,
So I am sitting here right now at home.
I haven't a clue what I am going to write,
My mind's a blank, could be here all night.
I am trying hard, the words won't come,
I must be thick as well as dumb.

I feel so daft I cannot think,
I'm sure tonight I'll not sleep a wink.
Then my inner self says 'Wake up mate,
Just get on with it and concentrate'
So I put the paper to my pen,
Lo and behold! What happened then?

Words came and on paper swiftly flew,
They filled my mind and quickly grew.
I could see everything clear at last,
My confidence rose, doubts in the past.
I became so wonderfully inspired,
Then went to bed pleasantly retired.

Errol A Johnson

BURNT-OUT SHELL

Once we had money and wealth
Now we have none
Once we had sunshine that has turned to rain and snow
Once we had flowers in bloom
Now they have withered away
Once we had fine clothes that have turned to rags
Once we had fame and fortune
That has gone away
Once we had love that has turned to anger
Once we had laughter that has turned to tears
Once we talked all day
That has turned to silence
Once we had many friends that now have gone away
Once we knew each other
Well, now we are strangers to each other in separate lives
Once we made love all night
Now, we have separate rooms
All that is left of life and love is a
Burnt-out shell.

Geoff Beatty

THROUGH THE EYES OF A CHILD

If we could look through the eyes of a child
We would see the world and be quite beguiled
A globe full of love and peace and pure joy
Shining from the heart of each girl and boy

Their world full of secrets yet to unfold
Mysterious stories yet to be told
For a child is a candle with eyes burning bright
To light up the way as we travel through life

A child feels no anger, no malice, nor fear
For their lives are more precious with each brand new year
They live for today and not for tomorrow
And have lives full of love with no pain and no sorrow

A child sees no colour when they make a friend
They are blind to all prejudice, right to the end
They never make judgements, they only can see
A world with equality, as was meant to be

We must make this world a much better place
In our hands it is true that we hold their fates
Through the eyes of our children it is sure we will see
The way that the world is intended to be.

Kathleen Christine Bennett

ONE SET SHY, THE OTHER MOCKING

It happened, just like that
Impeccable bonding
Two pairs of eyes locked together
One set shy, the other mocking

But the stage was set
The mocking eyes, the palest shade of grey
Held the shy ones hypnotised
Unable to tear away

Closer to each other they moved
Slowly across the crowded room
Until no more than a foot apart
Eyes still transfixed through the gloom

The beginning of a great love affair
By two pairs of eyes locking
Impeccably bonded
One set shy, the other mocking.

Anne Logan

PHOTO BOOTH

Keeping still, trying not to move.
Settled down comfortable in a photo booth
Hair is combed back neatly
Half smile upon the face
        There's a click from the camera
        And a bright flashing light.

Photo's been taken, stool's at the wrong height

Seat adjusted correctly, got it right at last
Look straight into the lens now
Did someone just go past?
Pulled back the curtain, gave a loud scream
Jerked my head round quick, no one to be seen
        There's a click from the camera
        And a bright flashing light.

Do I really look that awful when taken from the right?

A photo for my passport is all that I want
Sat there just waiting, looking straight in front
What's this funny feeling? Suddenly I freeze
Nose begins to tickle, out comes noisy sneeze.
        There's a click from the camera
        And a bright flashing light.

Face all crumpled up, I look such a fright.

I am getting up to leave now
Photo booths are not for me
Think I'll holiday in England
Still lots of sights to see
        There's a click from the camera
        And a bright flashing light.

Must stick to my arrangements, I'll still be on that flight.

V A Coulson

BLINDED

Grains of sand in a heart of stone
My turn to walk and yours to phone
The picture says that the piece won't fit
Your turn to walk and mine to sit

Cover my eyes in a shade of grey
Hide my thoughts in games you play
It's over soon it won't take long
You get to hear a poor man's song

Think of days with a darkest night
Then find a reason to search for light
And what scared you to make you hide
The love and hate that stirs inside

To stumble blindly on the ground
Where answers come but never found
Questions start at a journey's end
A cold sea lies but still no friend.

Lee Connor

IF

A heart that cries many tears
And faces the truth without delay
Need not be afraid to show its fears
If the strong don't run away

A sharp mind of captivating wit
With gentle grace and beauty that shines
Every day the truth proves worth it
If they glorify other minds

A man who takes life as it is
And takes the happiness with the pain
Will truly feel what is Heaven's kiss
If happy innocent tears stain

If answers we seek remain unfound
If fog covers truthful lies
If laughter shadows the sadness bound
Then why bother with goodbyes?

Graham Connor

St Valentine's Day

I find You in the clear, blue sky,
Wafting thunderclouds quite by,
To give assurance, not alone
Am I. I have You for my own,
A guardian so kind to me.
You rule the land, You stir the sea,
Informing me, to sail there
Is safe . . . You have me in Your care.

You look down from the heavens above.
You're my Valentine . . . a love
Of You possesses me today,
For You help me meet the fray,
Proposed to me by one or two,
Who may not know, I have You, true . . .
As true to me, Lord God, as ever
Lasts . . . desert me, Jesus, never!

Charles Hardman

SIGHTS OF SPRING

The sunlight in the morning
That flickers through the trees,
With fragrant apple blossom
Floating gently on the breeze,
A skylark flies high on the wing
His shrill song you'll hear him sing.

The ripples on the water
As the river trickles by,
The glisten of the sunshine
From a clear and cloudless sky,
A bumblebee on meadow flowers
Collecting pollen for hours and hours.

And in the fields along the lane
See newborn lambs at play,
Where sticky buds and catkins
Grace trees along the way,
The woodland is a haze of green
It really is a wondrous scene.

The sudden chill of evening
As the light begins to fade,
The hooting of a tawny owl
From a sleepy woodland glade,
Only sounds of wildlife calls
Break the silence, as the night-time falls.

The morning mist lies on the land
As dawn begins to break,
A hazy sun rises on the hill
To bring the sky awake,
A bird sings out to greet the morn,
As yet another day is born.

Maureen Reeves

LETTER FOR THE FUTURE

Letters, letters, I've written quite a few
And now I'm writing this especially for you
Let's look into the future for that's all we can do
Trying to cheer each other up, when we are feeling blue.

I listen every morning for that little rat-tat-tat
Followed by a letter dropping on the mat
I write to many people from all walks of life
They come from many countries where peace and war are rife.

I write to them of families and how they're getting on
Of those we've loved and cherished, and sadly now are gone
I tell them of my garden and the things that I am growing
Of my many varied hobbies such as writing, knitting, sewing.

The art of learning how to write
With pen and ink and paper
Is very much in the past
And like salt without its savour

I'm looking into the future
And wondering what I'll see,
There's an awful lot of gadgets
That really puzzle me.

There's Internet, dot coms
And a forward slash
It may make sense to you my friend,
To me it's simply trash!

Violet Cowley

AN ODE TO MARTY

Marty, Marty, now that you have flown
I reflect back on the many laughs we have known
Together with our care team on many outings to town
Remember the day we knocked those shoeboxes down?
Aunty Ann and Mam stacked them all up again
While you and I just couldn't stop laughing at them.

A fantastic sense of humour you always had
A remarkable young man and my smiley lad
You became over the past thirteen months or so
And on Saturday, 17th April, we had to let you go.

Sad times are ahead for us now you are gone
I promise you, Marty, I'll support Mam till she's strong
I was never only Marty's nurse, you know that's true
For Mam and Craig I have supported too
Loyal friends, we have learned to be
From strength to strength we'll go, you'll see

Remember our prayers said every night for you
For a sunny day and a smiley face that's true
Many tears I know are going to be shed
But sunny days and smiley faces, will come back instead

You are at peace my love with Nanna Flossie I know
She came to take you because it was your time to go
She'll take you and Oisheen to Heaven, that's for sure
For no one else in this world could be so pure
In love and laughter that glowed all around you
Like the heavenly angels that now surround you

God bless you now you are free from the pain
You have suffered so bravely but all in vain
A fight you could no longer take
This flight to Heaven you had to make.

Marie Gallagher

WHENEVER PEOPLE LOOK AT ME...

Whenever people look at me
Here's what I hope they really see:
Outrageously witty, funny and kind,
I sometimes shout but you shouldn't mind.
Racing around a badminton court
Everyone giggles because I'm quite short.
Always there for a little natter
Lately a lot but that doesn't matter.
Laughing at jokes and making some too,
Yes, *trying* to be funny is what I like to do!
Always willing to help someone out,
My friends are important; there's no doubt!

Lauren Allinson (11)

THE FARM

Are you going to the farm today
To cut the grass and make some hay;
To feed the pigs and the hens;
Collect the eggs and pack in tens;
To groom the horses with coats like silk;
To herd the cows and bottle the milk;
To clean the yard and dig the weeds;
To give the animals their feeds;
To build a silo for winter feed;
And plough the field to plant the seed?

When you've done the work required
I'm sure that you'll be feeling tired.
The day is over and it's getting late
When you leave the farm please shut the gate,
Cos if the animals escape into the lane -
The farmer won't let you go again.

Alan Tucker

UNTITLED

I know it's not shown often,
But still the feeling's there.
This feeling that I have for you,
A love beyond compare.

I have my moods but so do you,
And they sometimes meet head on,
But with love, it doesn't matter,
Who was right and who was wrong.

What I'm really trying to tell you
And I'm sure it shines clear through,
Is simple, my sweet love,
I'm so in love with you.

So if I lose my temper
Or you're feeling blue,
Just remember what I told you,
That our love will see us through.

D M Strange

My Grandson - Ethan Beard

Sent by God to give such joy
How good it feels to love this boy
Those trusting eyes gaze into mine
The bond between us feels so fine

Hands outstretched when I arrive
Throwing chippings picked up from the drive
I cradle his face in hands old and weak
And remove with finger, a tear from his cheek

Remembering the smile he gave everyone
Posing for photos and so full of fun
Looking in mirrors with side-on glance
In outsized hat and baggy pants

The mischievous smile he gave to me
Up the stairs we counted, 'One, two, three'

I visit the place where he used to live
Oh what joy, the memories give
Of moments together just him and me
Looking for 'diders' under the tree

All these things in my mind I can see
But oh how I wish he was nearer to me!

Terry Rowberry

THE BEAUTY OF GOD'S LOVE

A gilded sky, of glorious hues
A gently murmuring brook
A pair of softly shining eyes
Peer from a sheltered nook.
A lark soars singing high above
And with each note says, 'God is love.'

Beside the stream a thrushes' nest,
Among the treetops squirrels play,
In the woods where foxes hide,
And little rabbits whisk away.
There's where I love to sit and dream,
And let my thoughts drift with the stream.

And when the sun sails high above,
And fills the forest glades with light,
Each tiny floweret lifts its head,
An altogether lovely sight.
Then would I rest beneath the trees,
And listen to the whispering breeze.

At last the sun sinks down to rest,
And shades of night begin to fall.
I listen to the nightingale,
Whose lullaby steals over all.
Till even I would feign repose,
And let my weary eyelids close.

So as the silver moon rides high,
And sheds o'er all her silvery beam,
I wend my way now slowly home,
And wonder if it's all a dream
Of fairyland; and yet I know,
It's but God's love shown here below.

V P Lovell

REMEMBER

I'm thinking today
Of glory and shame
Of unsung heroes
We remember the name
Of those lest we forget
Who laid down their lives
For us - in their debt
One such was Michael
A young man in his prime
Always remember - take heed in time
Life can be short
Though days can be long
But memory is for ever
Theirs is the song
The boldest, the bravest
The flower of the land
For God and their country
Took up their stand
For a land fit for heroes?
Blameworthy indolent men!
Make a mockery of heroism
Selfishness reigns
Muggers - violators
Of God and of man
We've become a nation of cynics
But if we try we can
Remember our young men
They answered the call
For God and their country
They gave their all.

Jean Turner

LOVE OR POSSESSION?

Behold the call of nature, to beauty does it lend,
The male and female of every species each to other tend.
Voluptuous woman, a handsome man, it's just a common fact,
Colourful flowers, singing birds, born but to attract.
Wherever beauty dwells we notice sex involved,
The conservation of life itself, nature's mystery solved.
The lion in the jungle, the dove that flies above,
Man and woman just the same but we call it love.
A source of much blush cheeks the subject of taboo,
Tho' many talk and dwell we all enjoy to do.
Some fulfil their lust in realms of some subversion,
While few satisfy desires with acts of great perversion.
Whatever trends our leanings in the beddings,
A cunning fellow he who first thought of weddings.
Just sit, think and ponder and maybe analyse,
No need a piece of paper to gaze each other's eyes.
A being born to freedom till death us do part,
Tied by manmade reason, never to enamour another heart.
A mere legal mangle turned by society,
A possessive human tangle to maintain propriety.
A silly ceremony with very little merit,
So whatsoever one may possess, the other will inherit.
Did he never wonder nor stop to reason why?
From puberty feels many moods, till it's time to die.
So tho' in ecstasy as he makes his vows,
Didn't bargain for many years of loud and bitter rows.
Why did he dabble to rule nature's course?
Human freedom gamble, that endeth in divorce.

Al Môn

SPRING

Oh! How I long for spring to appear
With the first show of snowdrops, a sign that it's here!
Bare trees come alive, with green buds shooting through,
It's a season so fresh, and delightfully new!
Light showers of rain, to bring forth the flowers,
Cherry blossoms of white, clinging onto the boughs,
Thousands of daffodils in all shades of gold,
Giving pleasure to all, it's a joy to behold!
Catkins and sticky buds, sprays of palm,
Lovers strolling, arm in arm,
Lambs skipping about, play and nudge one another,
Then a sharp bleat! A warning cry from their mother!
The song of the bird, busy building its nest,
This is Mother Nature at her very best!
What more could one want, to feel like a king?
It's a wonderful medicine, a good dose of spring!

P McIlquham

THE PERFECT FRIEND

Although I'm on my own I'm not alone
I have one perfect friend to call my own,
And though my sight is dim Your smile I see;
Each day, dear Lord, You come and talk with me,
And though I'm deaf, Your tender voice I hear;
Dear Lord, with You I know I've naught to fear,
If my poor feet should stumble on life's road,
You'll come to me and gently take my load -
You'll take my hand in Yours and lead me on,
While You are near all cares will soon be gone.
It matters not where in this world I go -
If You are there, dear Lord, I'm safe - *I know.*

Eleanor Knipe

I Love Him All The Same

My girlfriends don't seem to like him
He's not playing by their rules
But I know he's too smart for them
'Cause he doesn't suffer fools
He knows what's important
He knows what love's about
And I want to tell the world
Stand on the roof and shout
He's not like the guys in the movies
He ain't no superstar
No flashy cars or credit cards
No escargot or caviar
To them he's not so special
Not much money and no fame
But none of that stuff matters
'Cause I love him all the same
He wears odd socks and jeans with rips
He doesn't care about fashion tips
His eyes light up when he smiles
For me, he'd walk a thousand miles
He smells so good, doesn't have to try
I look at him and my heart flies
So Jennifer can keep Brad Pitt
'Cause I've found love and my guy's it!

Zoë Margo Pearce

THE SOUNDS OF THE SEA

There are lots of beautiful things for me,
But I love to hear the rolling sea,
The seagulls crying from high above,
The crashing sound as the sea hits the rocks,
The laughter of children as they gather the shells,
The sea leaves behind after one of its swells,
The donkeys that trot up and down the sand,
With a tinkle of bells - what a lovely sound,
The rush of the lifeboat as it goes out to sea,
Keeping things safe for you and for me,
Yes I love the sound of the rolling sea,
Roll on, roll on, rolling sea.

T Smithies

WEATHER FORECAST

They're trundling out the covers at the Oval,
Start of play at Lords looks grim;
They're digging moats at Headingley,
And it's monsoon rain at Nottingham.
Old Trafford's under cloud, we hear,
And Hampshire's been called off;
Durham hasn't got a chance,
Sussex is already lost.
There's not a hope for Warwickshire,
And Worcester's almost drowned.
Essex is no better,
And there's bad light at Northants.
They've locked the gates at Derbyshire,
Glamorgan never stirred.
It's knee-deep at Grace Road,
And no one's heard a word from Kent.
Gloucester's one big puddle,
Somerset they say
Has sunk, so it's all just pouring rain,
You see, the miseries of county gloom,
Except in Little Thrusset
Where play starts prompt at noon.

Brian Parvin

AGAINST TERROR

I came, I saw, I conquered
So spake Caesar their Lord
Pursuing the ambition of ages
Conquest at the point of the sword

But what of the conquered I ask you
Were they to accept their changed lot
Now Roman cohorts were the new gang
To weave the Gordian knot?

Senators hailed him as 'Hero'
Progenitor Pax Romana
Historians awed by the glory
Acclaim Rome's ascent - Hosanna!

And what of Egypt and Persia?
Were they to care not a jot
That Rome was claiming its own turn
To weave the Gordian knot?

Were the Hun fighters for freedom
Or the vanguard of darkness and fear
Bringing to Europe more chaos
Or justice and liberty here?

So what of the enslaved and pillaged
Were their lives just spoilt to allot
Now Attila and his hordes imposed their right
To weave the Gordian knot?

A new source of order was needed
Claimed those with riches to lose
One constant you may be sure of
The governed had no right to choose

Was the Pontiff really a saviour
When into the saddle he got
And with every base machination
He too wove the Gordian knot?

The fear of brimstone was too weak
To halt the ambition of kings
And excesses of Rome goaded clerics
Protestants trying their wings

The common man may have cried freedom
But secession was just a dark plot
For imposing the dictates of new men
Who wove the Gordian knot

At last came the turn of plebians
The failings of rulers to mend
Having borne the wounds of their tyrants
Perhaps they'd get it right in the end

The dust of the great war not settled
And yet the lesson forgot
Nothing good ever greets those
Who weave the Gordian knot

So now we thrash ineffectually
In a web we have woven through time
All guilty by history's record
Of bloody internecine crime

Assaulting our brothers is facile
Their hope we must not garrotte
Long past is the moment we should stop
Weaving the Gordian knot

Steven J Smith

The Four-Year-Old

The child with the battered face,
No matter what breed or race,
Is tortured by unknown fear,
Is reduced to pathetic tears.
A sob in the quiet and dark,
Bruising of many a mark.
Crying alone, with no one to hear,
And steps on the stairs, they learn to fear.
Nobody can help, nobody knows,
Of that child's suffering and woe.

A stifled sob, never to hear anymore,
The enquiring knock at the door,
Muffled voices arguing in the hall,
Weeks pass, but nobody calls.

Summer passes through the window,
Catching her lying on the bed, pale and alone.
She moves to look down below,
At the drone of children laughing,
And cars moving in the distance.
Tears well up for the last time
As footsteps approach from below.

Winter blows against the window,
Rattling, battling, through day and night.
She does not hear this desperate sound,
She lies on the bed, resting, smiling.
Suffer little children into the arms of Jesus.
Bring her from the darkness into the light.
She's smiling now, her soul is burning bright
And she's found love forever and ever.

John Charles Porter

GOING HOME

The street's all clear
The sky's dark black
I don't know
If he'll be back.

He left me here
Cold and alone
Why won't someone
Come take me home?

A light in the distance
Is trying to see
I pray to God
They notice me.

Whose are the voices
Out there in the light?
A quire of angels
Singing in flight.

My spirit is soaring
My body is gone
Where am I going?
It's taken so long.

The anger has left me
My world's far below
Here is my new home
It's time to let go.

D Streek

AN ODE TO A MEMORY

I remember the day,
    When you stood by my side,
In the church,
    Wherein we were wed.

There was no need for words,
    For the shine in your eyes,
Was like a 'poem'
    That once I had read.

The thrill that I had,
    From that moment of bliss,
Was a joy,
    I shall cherish for e'er.

And I knew there and then,
    As you stood by my side,
That I'm glad it was 'I',
    That was standing there.

And although it's long past,
    Since that day, which was ours,
And the years
    May have taken their toll,

For the shine in your eyes has gone
    And our youth, this has flown,
But I still love you,
    Dear 'heart and soul'.

To recapture that moment,
    Would be a joy untold,
And would be a cure,
    To end all pain.

But alas, this may not be,
    For the time we can't turn,
But the memory,
    Will last not in 'vain'.

Sidney Dudson

THE WRATH OF MANKIND

We were put on this Earth for the good of mankind,
Little did we know what disasters we'd find,
From earthquakes to floods, famine and drought,
I'm beginning to wonder why it's all come about.
There's torture and murder, also children abused,
Down and outs sleeping in cardboard boxes, it's seen on the news,
We see soldiers fighting, it all ends in war,
There's always someone who needs to settle the score,
We have soccer hooligans, both home and abroad,
Juvenile delinquents who squirt paint on a wall,
Young joyriders who care for none but themselves,
Also drink and drunk drivers who put families through hell,
Old-age pensioners who are constantly mugged,
Often from people who are hyped-up on drugs,
There are both male and females we know them as 'gays',
Who eventually die from the catching of Aids,
But alas I'm afraid this is the price we now pay,
What's written above is merely manmade,
We must accept that the world is now in decline,
There's only one factor to blame, that's the wrath of mankind,
Until the greed and the selfishness all disappear,
We can no longer walk the streets without any fear.

S Tranter

SEARCHING FOR MAGIC

People may disconcert you, and proceed to tell you that,
Magic is just an ancient myth, like rabbits out of hats.
But scientists so far, even with rockets and laser beams
Have missed all the vital signs, as to what this adjective means.

And through all of history's wonders, like Egypt and World War II,
Only handfuls of special people, recognise its purpose and pursue.
But oh so many poets, in Britain and across the land,
Can tell you what it means, and let you understand.

They'll say, 'magic' is an autumn breeze across a crystal-clear lake,
Or listening to the sound of rain as you just start to wake.
It's rowing on a lake in British summertime,
And as you row you seem to lose all track of present time.

There are so many things that bring magic into view,
If you want to witness more, just try something new.
So remember the worldly magic around us is rife,
The true thing that matters inside is . . . life.

Mathew Watkins (14)

THE FALL

The sun goes down, a golden ball
The days grow short come the fall
The trees stand silent
All shades of brown
The leaves gently falling down
Shadows grow longer, days grow short
All is sad, summer is mort
Winter's waiting in the wings
With snow and ice and bitter winds
And there they stand, stark and bare
Till spring is in the air
And from the earth
Spring all shades of green
Where the cruel hand
Of winter's been.

Walter Sinclair

FREE

Lullaby world ultimate sleep
Intense smiles comfort gone
Beneath splendour choices free
Innocent memories casually glide
Tender logic softly enfolding
Sublimely shivering watchful glances.

Maria Riccardi

My Beloved

The love of my life has died,
But however I try to hide,
My grief will keep pouring out,
And I want to shout and shout.

Where are you my dearest?
How I wish you were nearest
To me as I sit all alone
In this house that was always our home.

In the twenty-seven years we were together,
We were seldom apart, almost never.
But now you have been taken from me
I find it hard to see.

The light has gone out of my life
We were as one, as husband and wife.
One day we will be reunited,
But until then my life will be blighted.

G Bryant

THE MIRACLE OF DAVID

The small child in his bed lay sleeping,
A tiny teddy for comfort he held tight,
The soft glow of a nightlight to protect him,
And make him feel safe through the night.

He knows his parents are close by him,
Watchful in case he awakes,
To hold him in his hours of slumber,
Reassuring him with each breath that he takes.

He was born into this world very early,
Premature and so incredibly small,
And with the dedication of the doctors and nurses,
It was a miracle he survived at all.

Soon it will be his first birthday,
To celebrate and rejoice,
Presents and cards to surprise him,
Sounds of happiness will be heard in his small voice.

His parents will always give thanks for their miracle,
And they will show it in the love that they give,
The little boy will always know his parents love him.

Their miracle . . . their own dear baby son so special . . .
They named him David.

Mary Plumb

DROUGHT

Sun-baked. Earth cracks
and mud splits its veins.

Disrobed. Soil is thirsty.
No water now for days.

Scorched. Cindered grass
turns to dust as we kneel

At its smouldering wake.
Flowers crackle and fall

Apart . . . limb from limb:
searching for their roots.

Parched tongues. Death
loiters in the air, as we

All move around in a slow
laboured motion. Only

Stone and shattered bone
will survive in this ash.

Louis Foley

A Vitriolic Romance

Knights on horses and ladies in corsets
Dark obsession can darken our doorsteps . . . forever

To turn things upside down can cause a frown
To love yet not to be in love you drown . . . completely

Radically we mix and match our tastes
We need so much we pant and salivate . . . hungrily

A simple soul can be so hard to find
We are always entangled in a bind . . . crazily

Affection quickly turns to rejection
Sex can so easily cause defection . . . utterly

It's now I see what it is to be free
But I do not want to be free from thee

Stick around, Love, please!

Elaine Borowski

SPRING

Green leaves are pushing
Through cold earth skywards
Pale yellow rays sifted by clouds
Beckon sleepy buds forth
Snowdrops hang fragile heads
Giving hope that
Spring will soon be here
Unexpected falls of snow freeze
Birdcall and struggling plants
Delaying their splendour and
Hope-giving properties
After the thaw, crocuses explode
In a riot of purples and yellows
Narcissi and daffodils advance
To match their colourful friends
New growth on hedgerows
Green leaves unfurling on boughs
A bitter wind challenges
Their right to be
Nature overcomes weather in the annual battle
Spring is here.

Sue Byham

Mummy

'Your mummy is going to be a mummy again,' my granny said to me.
'I know all about that,' I said, 'I learned about that in history.
They wrap you up in bandages, then soak your body in oils,
Then they bury you for thousands of years, then robbers come and
                                        steal your spoils.'
Last night I heard my mummy moan and groan.
I hid under my quilt cover, I could hear Daddy on the phone.
This morning my granny gave a whoop of delight,
Why is my granny so happy? My mummy became a mummy
                                        the other night!
Daddy is taking me and Granny to the hospital this afternoon,
I am quite surprised to be seeing my mummy quite so soon.
'Mummy, you've lost your bandages, and you're looking
                                        thinner today.'
'Come and see your baby sister, that I had while I was away.'
My baby sister is smashing, she's called Tamzin Ruth,
But I wish Mummy and Daddy had told me, told me the real truth.
Next year we're going to Egypt for our holidays.
We are going to see lots of mummies, and soak up the sun's rays.
My granny is still laughing, but there is something she doesn't know,
There are fairies in her garden, I've seen their footprints in the snow!

Emma Lockyer

The Gardener's Lot

'We plough the fields and scatter
The good seed on the land'
   And . . .
The land is flooded -
Germination is delayed -
Spring flowers late displayed
But then, there is a glimpse of sun
A warming of the soil,
The gardener starts to toil.

Bugs, slugs and crawling grubs
The garden lover's nightmare,
Green fingers out there, lots of care;
The leaves appear and then the buds
And then the aphids; earwigs
Scream . . .
An ecologist's dream!

Grown men and women
Grub in the soil,
The grass grows quickly - endless mowing.
Hours of backache, hours of toil.
First the digging and then the sowing
Followed by shoots and then the stem -
Amen.

The weather's perfect, the crops mature
Seasons changing, harvest in
And then again the work begins.
Autumn digging, plus manure
A brief respite during winter's gloom,
A choice of seeds in the living room
And then . . .

Yvonne Bulman Peters

By Moonlight

Casting its icy glow, the moon shines so bright.
Stars are now twinkling, flowers shut tight.
Flickering shadows lure the fox from his lair,
Breath comes in sharp puffs of white on the air.
Unreal is the field in this fantasy world,
Dew on the sheep wool so tightly curled
Where it hangs, caught on the barbed wire spike
When they reach too far for the ivy they like.
Frost is now glistening upon the sheep coats.
They lie very still save for movement of throats
As they sleepily doze, munch and chew on their cud.
The warmth of their bodies melts frost into mud.
Footsteps are crunching on grass blades now lost,
Stiffened and whitened by cruel fingers of frost
As a coating settles upon the clear air,
Everything's dressed in cold sparkling wear.
Icicle sculptures push up, grow and form
Between leaves on the floor, till the sun starts to warm.
Then they fall and they drip and they just run away
As the frost disappears with the sunlight of day.

Wendy Simpson

The Symbolic Tree

Majestically he climbs, while knarled twisted
Branches hungrily find, fading dances of the sun.
Wind and rain pound relentlessly upon wrinkled bark,
Suppressing groaning, in the oncoming dark.

Undaunted, still he stands, majestic against night's sky,
Defying the elements, his existence to deny.
Words are unspoken, but somewhere inside
He knows there is purpose, to heavenward climb.

His knarled twisted branches and wrinkled bark,
Have earned him experience, and an all-knowing heart.
By weathering the storms with patience and care,
A character emerges, both humble and rare.

Muriel Billyard Bond

A Message For Dad

You gave me life, you and Mum created me
You brought me up to be the best that I could be
You made me smile; you wiped my tears away
You're in my heart and my mind every single day
I believe you are watching over my family and me
And I know you will always go on loving me
I was proud to call you Dad and walk by your side
You were that special person in whom I could confide
I will never stop loving you for as long as I live
I trust and believe in you just like I always did
I know you will listen whenever I talk
I know you are beside me wherever I walk
You will always be here in my heart
So we shall never be far apart
My love for you will never wane
God bless you Dad till we meet again.

Amanda Stredwick

THE FISHERMEN
(Written on the 5th April 2004)

I awake at 6am, the same time as the sun is about to rise,
The mist is clearing, leaving behind beautiful clear blue skies,
The sea is calm, with fishing boats making their way to trade,
Taking fish from nets, before they arrive at harbour, seeing how much
they've made.
The tranquillity in the dawn light, made by the dedicated few,
A tradition since time itself, as old as morning dew,
These men of the sea, weather-beaten, fearless and brave,
Just sit there on their way to market, a tradition they try to save,
The colourful boats, painted yellow, blue and red,
Until the fishermen, like their fish, all end up dead,
And then their sons repaint their boats, and hope for a full and
profitable catch,
As the years pass on by, Dad and Grandad they try to match,
Just for us to have our fish, fried or grilled,
With bellies full, all satisfied and filled,
Spare a thought for these brave souls of the sea,
The ones who fight the elements for our tea,
Raise your glass, and offer a toast, to the men so strong,
Again at dusk, there they go, into the night so long.

T J Styles

The Reality Of War

We see the look of sadness
Engraved on everyone's face.
We see the deprivation
And destruction of this place.
What once was a beautiful city
Is now just deserted streets.
Where people dodge the bullets
Just to find something to eat.
Their homes have turned to rubble
The smell of death hangs in the air.
Their bodies are empty shells now
Motionless they just sit and stare.
For they have lost everything
They've no strength to fight anymore.
It's an effort just to survive now
This is the reality of war.
The innocent are the losers
All they want is to be free.
All they have now are their memories
Of how life used to be.
The picture shows a small child
Down his cheek there rolls a tear.
The only childhood memories he'll have
Are ones that are filled with fear.
Thousands of lives are ruined
It's an expensive price to pay.
For in war there are no winners
I hope peace will come one day.

Amanda Jayne Hibbert

The Visitor

I fell in love with an alien, who came from outer space,
She had two eyes of deepest blue and one as white as lace.
She had one ear, elephant's size, that tapered till it pointed,
A zippered mouth in the middle of her forehead and a nose that was double jointed.
She had three legs but just two arms, although it must be said,
One grew from her shoulder and one grew from her head.
She had nice breasts on her back which made them look quite false,
They didn't help her jumper's shape but were great when we did the waltz.
Her hair was so long and soft it hung down like golden thread,
Under her arms, on her face, but none on top of her head.
She had nine fingers on each hand or ten if you count her thumbs,
And could play a duet with herself on piano and the drums.
We've tried to talk and communicate but still not had much luck,
For when her spaceship crashed to Earth her zipper got well and truly stuck.
This could also cause problems eating so you would suppose,
But she siphons food through a straw straight up into her nose.
I've heard them say that beauty is in the eye of the beholder,
So when her third leg fell off, it was me who applied the solder.
I know she's not good-looking like the conventional English rose,
And she's probably not the daughter-in-law my parents would have chose,
But I am going to marry her, she fills me with such pride,
And when we lay down together only one arm digs in my side.
So we gathered outside the church on our special day,
But in the high winds our photographer began to sway.
He said if I could ask the bride to lend a helping hand,
I'm sure with her three legs she'd make a perfect tripod stand.
We finally stood at the altar, our vows about to say,
When a great shaft of light flashed and beamed my alien love away.

Len Mann

THE LOSS OF A LOVED ONE

Death comes to catch us unaware.
It hits at the hearts of those who care.
We hurt, we weep, we mourn, we grieve,
And still we find it hard to believe,
Our loved one's gone, no more 'to be',
Except a beloved memory,
But time will pass and soon we'll find,
Feelings of a different kind.
We'll be happy and we'll laugh and sing,
But we'll not forget, just a word can bring
. . . a memory, a thought, a face,
Until we meet in that special place.

Myria Hayers

FILL THAT SPACE

A time to heal, a time to bless,
There is no place to run a mess,
For I have come to save your soul,
To lift you and bless and fill your nest

There is no time to run and hide,
For I am here to take your pride,
Come and share the gift of life,
To run amok is all but strife

There is no time but present need,
Oh come, I say, and share my grace,
To fill that space and comfort thee.

Amen

D Ierotheou

WORLD OF PEACE

We all hope for peace in our world today
As we kneel together and we pray
May our own faiths light up our darkest hours
And lift up our heart to their healing powers

May we be faithful in every way
Always, always, not for just a day
In our own beliefs we all trust
But the downfall of our neighbours
We should not lust

Show love for our brothers
No matter what creed
For love and honour should always succeed

May our lives be filled with all kinds of love
As we seek salvation from above
Our lives are short so let's make them good
Deep in our hearts we know we should

Life is worth living, come what may
Working together can make the sun shine every day
Love and tolerance, we must make room
Living from the heart will lift the gloom

Just what's happening to the human race?
Why can't we make the world a better place?
Don't let our lives just fall apart
Can't the world live life from the heart?

G Breakspear

A World Gone Mad

Through the years changes have taken place,
Some for better, some for worse, depending on the case.
Changes in the law of the land, but are they for the best?
Trading on the Sabbath, which should be a day of rest.

There's conflict around the world, and strife throughout the land,
Soldiers die doing their duty in the heat of the desert sand,
To free a people from tyranny and give them peace and hope,
But war is a harsh reality, some say they shouldn't have gone . . .
Is freedom and peace worth fighting for? Yes! That's why they're
                                                                                                                                                          battling on.

We query the injustice, immigration, lack of care.
The overcrowded prisons and . . . drug pushers from who knows where.
Waiting lists for operations, budget cuts for schools,
Is it really lack of money . . . or are we being fooled?

Now spare a thought for our children, some already using dope.
With pressure and strife, ruling their life, they reckon there's no hope.
The TV isn't much better, it's full of sex and crime,
Surely there's a much better way, to help our kids use their time?

No one is safe, whether on street, or at home,
With rapists, muggers, thieves out for gain, targeting the vulnerable
                                                                                                                                                                         living alone.
Why . . . is this world full of hatred and pain?
With road rage, murder, and porn on the net,
The police are not winning, how much worse can it get?

Crime receives little punishment, but is it the correct way?
Justice demands a price to be paid, on that great Judgement Day.
So what of our world and the mess it's in?
All I can say, it's all down to sin.

A special prayer for society today,
Is to know God's grace! His commandments to obey.
May the news in the papers be, a reflection of kind,
That gives hope to our hearts and peace to our minds.

R A Hinson

JUST THINK ABOUT IT

I just can't conceive
What goes on in the mind
Of fools who light fires
And the mess left behind.
They destroy our lush forests
Spreading *death* on our land
Making all wildlife leave
Or just burn where they stand.
They give no concern
To the damage that's done
They seem to ignore
All the creatures they've harmed.
The wildlife all leaves
All the birds take their flight
Leaving miles of our country
With nothing in sight.
So to all of the *idiots*
Who don't stop to think,
Before burning our mountains
Making wildlife extinct,
Please take a moment
Just stand back and see
You're hurting the wildlife,
The forest and *me!*

Dai Jon Maddocks

LOVE NEVER DIES

Looking out of my window,
Trying to work out how it could be so,
Sweet memory comes to me in a dream,
Now I want to redeem,
All those mistakes that I freely made,
And in happiness break down the barricade,
Because just as the summer sun will always rise,
Love never dies,

Watching her hair,
Remember how much we used to share,
Made me feel like a little boy,
In her eyes I found a joy,
Enough to make me forget the tears,
Enough to make me forget the fears,
Because just as the summer sun will always rise,
Love never dies,

Wake up early in the morning,
For her sweet breath I'm still yawning,
Knowing that she belongs to the past,
Wondering for how long this feeling will last,
If you see me cry,
Know there's more to the tears in my eye,
Because just as the summer sun will always rise,
Love never dies,

In her eyes I see something,
That says she, too, is missing,
The warm, sunny days,
The lazy, carefree ways,
It's a love that will always exist,
Like the memory of a first kiss,
Because just as the summer sun will always rise,
Love never dies.

Karl Wade

OUR ALBERT'S A VIP

Our Albert's Lord Mayor now, 'e was appointed t'other day,
It's a far cry from 'is other job, wheel tapper on't railway.
'e was picked by the lads on't council, townsfolk didn't hear a whisper,
'til a picture appeared in't local paper of Albert with 'is eldest sister.

She's got the job of Mayoress tha knows, cos our Albert never got wed;
'e didn't waste 'is time like t'other lads, 'e went t' pub instead.
'e looks proper posh when 'e's all dressed up, with 'is chain of office danglin',
Albert don't like that chain, cos when it goes dull 'e's got to polish the thin'.

Now 'e goes t' local operatic shows and them classical concerts too,
Albert don't understand them at all but it's 'is job and the thing to do.
'e opens fêtes and jumble sales and collects crowds wherever 'e goes,
Tha folk don't come t' see Albert but it's smart t' be seen with the Mayor, tha knows.

Hobnobs with all the suave gentry and ladies with small evening bags;
'e's out of 'is depth when the chat begins but when the suppin' starts 'e never lags.
You'll see our Albert at every big 'do', eatin' chicken and drinkin' red wine,
The way the folk applaud 'is speeches you'd think 'e were bloody Einstein!

Albert makes big decisions now, though 'e's only a little fella,
'course he's 'elped by the lads on't Council, especially by Seamus O'Kella.
Now 'e used to be a navvy on't roads of 'is native Eire;
But rumour 'as it 'e's after the job of next Lord Mayor.

Our Albert's term of office ends, 'round about March '63,
'e'll 'ave 'ad enough be then, but that's between thee and me.
Then it's back to 'is old job that 'e did every day;
With a keen ear and a 'ammer, tappin' wheels on't railway.

Brian Denton.

GROWING UP

When I was young and just aged three
No one could tell how life would be
My days were filled with games to play
I didn't want for anything to pass the time of day.

I had my toys, my friends and pets, my brother and sister too
To play and skip without a care and loads of things to do.
And when I cried or things seemed such a muddle
It wasn't long before my mum gave me a kiss and cuddle.
I had all that when I was small, a bright and happy home
A caring mum and family, to never feel alone.

And then the day I started school was really quite traumatic
For I was used to being free, the days were quite erratic.
And when I reached my teenage years the world was at my feet
When I could choose and please myself and loads of friends to meet.
My days were filled with exciting things, ambitions to come true
With thoughts of travel here and there and lots of things to do.

My jobs I had were not too bad, although at times consuming
I had to be there right on time or else the boss was fuming.

And when my teenage years had passed and I had settled down
To married life and stability and children of my own,
I cannot believe how time has passed, and how they all have grown.
They too have dreams and plans of sorts, and children of their own.
They look to me as I do to Mum, who to us, is our greatest fan.
To me she's my mum, and will always be, and to my children their
favourite nan.

Jean Yates

POOR OLD SOUL

Well done! You've lasted one more year.
I don't believe it, you're still here!
You've got new glasses, more false teeth:
I've put on hold that funeral wreath.

The doctor thinks you're in good health,
Has no concern for your vast wealth.
But does he care, when you complain
Of fluid loss and stomach pain?

I know you've nothing much to fear:
You've cut out cigarettes and beer.
And that step-counter on your belt
Will help that extra weight to melt.

Keep polishing your Zimmer frame,
Make sure that guide dog's on its chain.
But, if you think you might collapse,
Don't let your insurance lapse.

Please, take these thoughts from your good mate:
Don't whinge and whine, life is still great.
So, just stay healthy, free from ills,
And keep on taking all those pills!

Brian M Wood

TERRORISTS STRIKE AGAIN

On Thursday, 11th March in Spain,
Terrorists murder and maim again.

In train carriages the bombs they hid,
And innocent commuters were blasted.

Minds are numb,
Mouths struck dumb.

Live TV in on the scene,
The carnage is obscene.

People hug their loved ones with relief,
Or wait for news that ends in grief.

Three days of mourning are declared,
One nation's deep distress is shared.

Outside the station, flowers make a shrine,
Candles are lit and in the darkness shine.

What organisation could be to blame?
It doesn't matter, as they feel no shame!

Rosemary Davies

YOU THERE
(In that chair!)

Have you ever been abused?
Do you feel that you've been used?
Are you one who feels 'alone'?
Do not be there just to moan
Can you not carry that 'heavy' load?
Do you feel that a life you're owed?
Does *disabled* fill the bill?
Do you feel a prisoner still?
Though you may be handicapped
It is *you* who is making 'you' trapped
Though dependent on your chair
There *is* a future for you out there
There is a life for you to find
Stop that whining - (I do not mean to seem unkind)
You see *I* am *disabled* too
But I do express my points of view
Have you chatted with those who've cared?
Are you of 'authority' scared?
Must you feel sorry for yourself?
It's time to climb down off that shelf
You are but handicapped - *not* insane
Why not now start using that brain?
You will find that that 'rod' bends
Invite others to be your friends
Cut those bonds that hold you tight
'Stand up' now and hardship fight
Why should *you* on *others* depend
When it is *you* who should your message send?
'Off those backsides onto feet
Your own handicap - *now defeat!*'

John El Wright

LIKE SAINT PETER, LEARNING

One Jesus morning
blessed house martins building -
stones sing in gardens,
sweet and rough rock salty,
like Saint Peter, learning.

You'll be that some summer
if you swoop to listen -
allowing seeing's stoop
to sweep much steeper
flights of head

Then, if you notice,
stones hand your spirits flowers
by the fistful in your thinking -
and other Jesus mornings
with sparrows building sermons
through each season of the year

That speak even in tenfoots
sowing urinated mattress
where old fridge blossom opens
which you'll notice as your mind swoops
to taste such sweet salts there -

Whilst walking through the valleys
of overflowing dustbins,
tears swooping from your head low
let a sad child's watery smile know
you've noticed Jesus denied
in his mother's stooping eyes.

Peter Asher

VEGETARIANS VERSUS MEAT EATERS
(There are at least two sides to everything)

Vegetarians look at sheep and cattle in the fields
And say, 'How can anybody kill and eat them?'
I can understand this feeling for I don't like the idea of slaughter
But I like eating meat, so what are the alternatives?

We travel the countryside and see the sheep and cattle in field after field
Looking healthy, fed and cared for by the farmers
Would vegetarians feed and care for them and pay for vets
when needed?
No, it's money that we pay for meat, part goes to the farmers

To care and look after them and there are many easier ways to make
a living
So there would not be any sheep or cattle in the fields but for the
meat eaters
You may find a few in zoos or someone may keep one as a pet
Or perhaps we may have viewing farms where you would pay to
see them

Now we come to the slaughter of the animals that I don't like
the idea of
Most would have had a good healthy life, the alternative is to let them
die of old age
Would you remove the corpses from the fields or bury or burn them?
Most meat eaters create a life for animals, although limited -
vegetarians deny life to millions.

Keith Jackson

STORMS

There is always a storm
Somewhere on this place called Earth.
There are the storms of sea,
There are the storms of time,
There are the storms of sand,
There are the storms of earth, wind and fire,
But most of all . . .
There are the storms of *life*,
For without life,
What need would there be for 'storms'?

Jean Donne

WHISPER INSIDE A BROKEN CHILD

Does anybody hear the wind chimes?
The cry of a child in the cold?
The sands of time that are rolling
But I that never grow old?

Does anybody feel the night?
The ice that sings on the ground?
The ten thousand hearts that are beating
But never make a sound?

Does anybody think of the spirits?
The ghosts that hide in every tree?
The whisper inside a broken child?
Someone exactly like me.

Does anybody know who I am?
Does anybody even care?
I stand in the dusty hallway, crying.
To those who are never there.

Does anybody watch the stars?
Does anybody read the Milky Way?
I wish that you could hear me.
But that is all I can say.

Jasmyn Galley (11)

COLOURS

There's a
Rainbow
That you
Can chase

All the
Colours of
The race

So chase
That rainbow
In the sky

And let
Not life
Pass you
By.

Tim Johnson

WHO IS GOD?

God is an ocean of love, kindness and mercy
and He flows through the entire universe
regardless of caste, creed or faith.

God exists in various forms and is worshipped in
different ways in many countries.

Whatever the faith or religion, the final goal is
to seek and try to understand God and the
paths may vary but the ultimate destination is one.

The question asked is why there is so much sorrow,
misery and tragedy in this world if God is so loving
kind, caring and considerate?

These are not God's actions or responsibility but
people's own greed, hate, jealousy and love of
material things.

Life is full of temptations and the path to God is
filled with various obstacles or hurdles.

If one can still pursue the ultimate goal despite
all prevailing difficulties and worldly pleasures,
one will be a step closer to God.

I sincerely hope and pray that one day we
shall find God and true inner happiness.

K R Kadkol

THE STREET WITH NO NAME

As I walked round this part of town
I found some very strange houses,
They were almost falling down.

There are streets like this in every town
I think they are more at the seaside.
Behind the glitz and glamour, just out of sight
You will find the homes of no-hopers
And you'll look and wonder in fright
And think, 'Could this be me in time to come
When I am old and have lost my pride?'
But look again, there are young people too
Who haven't a hope about life.
When money's short and times are hard
Not much food or warmth, just a room in an
Old, old house to keep you from the storm.
You look at the shops you can't afford,
No wonder so many windows are boarded.

You go to the pub for that one lonely drink
Make it quick, you might get in a fight.
The children, too, what a life
Just fighting and pushing around,
No gardens, no toys, just old, old houses,
Waiting to fall down.

You could walk to the sea if you had some shoes,
But be afraid you might throw yourself in.
So I walk away, no, I don't, I run,
I'm going to find my place in the sun.
A street with a name!

Jocelyne Trickett

The Monument

Civic pride is everywhere
Precarious in park or square.
Elements have wrought a deep patina
Upon the marbled worthies.
Yet weathered stone shares this
With the fugitives from hostile streets
The fragile content of a cardboard box.

A cruel nuance marks the Bohemian.
Whilst marbles wax, flesh rots -
The legends of stone are harder than bone;
The niche that is given is mortal.
The man who is lost is finally found
Wrapped in newsprint, leaves and shred -
A statue to be unwrapped when dead?

'Yet for legend as for myth
Man might count as marble.
That contemporary monument
As yet unveiled - invites
The pigeon - white to mark him
As the latest roost
Amongst the honoured reliquaries.'

William Birtwistle

Our Multicultural World

What is the difference between you and me?
We both have a family, can't you see?
They're always there to love and care
When I was alone, they gave me a home.

We don't share the same race
Because I'm from a different place
They taught me to lead a good life
And now I'm a wife

My husband is the one I lean upon
He keeps me strong when things go wrong
People stare but we don't care
The love is there because of the things we share

We fight through things
And we face what life brings
It's not about the colour of our face
We share our feelings face to face

So what is the difference between you and me?
Apart from our colour, there's nothing I can see!

Jane Limani

What Do You Do?

What do you do
When you're nearly two
And people stop
And stare at you?

Do you sit and grin,
Or try to sing?
Do you cry for your mum
Or bang a drum?
What do you do?

Do you stand up tall
Or walk in the hall?
Do you try to eat
Or kick with your feet?
What do you do?

Put your arms up high,
Try and reach for the sky,
Or lie down flat
On your tummy or back?
What do you do?

I'm nearly two.
I know what I'll do
When people stop to stare at me.
I'll suck my dummy
And look for my mummy.
That's what I'll do.

D E Hampshire

FATE IS GREAT

Once . . . in a blue moon
You notice changes happen in your life.
Fate drags you nearer and nearer
To the strife which you'd like to cut with a knife . . .

To define fate
How can it be done?
The greatness of your own fate
Makes your life a whole one . . .

Times can get rough
Thanks to fate
It can also make you late
For a romantic date . . .

Without fate
Where would we all be?
Certainly not on Earth
Being scrutinised by all this democracy . . .

Fate is great
Even if you disagree,
What you can't ignore
Is that it creates your destiny . . .
As you will soon see . . .

Darren Protheroe

SCREAMING FRIENDS' PURSUIT

Red dew clusters the roses.
They weep in solitude
Little bits of petals torn to lead
Gone the joy, gone the pain of their torment
On stones they crack shortened to a thousand pieces
If you knew what I have heard
You would not want to know,
Angels in their glory,
Masters in the snow,
Cold is the night as its shadows rip the night,
In fright tomorrow may not come.

A regiment of misery is lying in the snow,
Can we love, it is hard to know
When someone will never let you go.

Marie Jones

LIVE LIFE

Have you looked into the face of a cat
And wondered what it is thinking about?
Its inscrutable stare as it looks into space
Probably laughing at the human race.
We run ourselves silly day after day
To work till we drop, our bills to pay
Do we stop in the clamour of the day
To smell the blossom or sweet hay?
Pause to listen to the song of a bird
A truly wonderful sound to be heard.
Take time to meet and talk with a friend
Laugh and remember all the good times we had.
Life is such a hectic pace and rush
We forget all the little things that mean so much
That makes life so precious and worthwhile
To give us the reason to stand and smile
That whatever the future has to hold
With the love of a friend we can resolve
Any difficulties thrown our way
So we can each and every day
Be enjoying life's challenges whatever we get
We can really envy the way of a cat
Be honest, faithful, loving and true, that is all that is demanded of you.

Jeanette Styles

IN THE END
(To a boy who was bullied to death)

I don't know . . .
Maybe at the end of some rainbow
All such kids - like you meet
Maybe now life - for you
For the first time is sweet.

For in this world - it was not.
You were left to rot.
Headaches - with too much work.
Kids like you -
Circled out as a welcome 'jerk'.

Then you got counselling - 'Think positive!'
Maybe now - you could live.
But to whom could your little soul turn
When reality, darkness
Took its turn . . . ?

Who was there - who would care?
God - for one - wasn't there.
Who the f**k was aware
That you -
No more could take this daily hell . . . ?

I guess all your murderers -
Young and old - sleep well.

Johannes Robert McCormack

THE FIELDS OF TIBET

As we walked across the fields of Tibet,
We cradled our weapons, we embraced the dead,
More rigid than steel and nobler than stone!
That is what a good man said,
As we walked across the fields of Tibet.

We hunted for paradise cradling our weapons,
Embracing the dead in search for silence.
We should have died a long time ago,
But now we are here and free,
In the green fields of Tibet.

I have this post-apocalyptical dream,
When the human mind exceeds its limitations,
And ventures to the boundary again.
On this occasion, one is not afraid to break the umbilical cords,
Which connect him to the world as he understands it.

As I taught him how to dance
And stare straight into the sun!

We were happier in forgetful times.
When the starlings returned for spring,
There was a celebratory tone in the air,
As we walked across the fields of Tibet.

We were searching for somewhere to sleep
And we were looking for somewhere to die,
In the fields of Tibet.

D Johnson

THE COOK

Is that the sweet smell of your cooking, my dear
For a little more fat on my body, I fear
By the smell, I will eat it with relish, I'm sure
When I've emptied my plate I will come back for more
Without doubt you're the best little cook that I know
The aromas you cause make the saliva flow
You're an expert at finding your way to my heart
I go hungry a lot, the sad times we're apart
I wait and I starve until your return
For a plate of your cooking, I yearn, how I yearn!
I really don't care I put weight on each day
For the pleasure you give, it's a small price to pay
So finish your cooking with taste and with speed
For my nose, it tells me, I'm to get a good feed.

G Andrews

A Chicken To Pluck

The chicken was scatting, around in the run
Survived torrents, winds, and the fiery sun
It was picked, caught and carried away
With wings flapping, eyes alert, this was the day
Just out of sight, its neck broke in a pull
Ambitious in rearing, not so much with the cull
First time for everything, this'll do me no harm
My stomach churning, clasped meat with some charm
Some dust shook about as I raised it by feet
Flopped it purposefully on laps, to ensure it looked neat
I plucked at the feathers, glossy each one
I couldn't stop now, there was a job to be done
Onlookers stared, as I was going so slow
Timing my plucking, with a long way to go
I got a bit confident and lifted its head
The neck was all floppy, eyes shut meant it dead
I continued around feeling feathers and skin
Glared at the flesh now looking so thin
The skin was tugged hard, going back and forth
No time for sentiments, its soul had gone north
Many feathers escaped, as I was filling a bin
I eat supermarket meat, this is not such a sin
If this was so bad, there was much worse to come
As I tugged its insides and emptied its tum
Feathers still stuck to it, here and there
Reminded me that I still couldn't share
The skin I removed, with a stretch like elastic
It was nice to think organic, was nothing like plastic
Lovingly fed and fresh water each day
Just eating and lazing, not really at play
The run still looks full, another cock takes its place
Well fed and content, to them it's no race
The giblets all cooked, the portions are cut
I chose this lifestyle to get out of a rut

As I show off my tray, cleaned chicken with pride
It meant admitting, my organic chicken once died
The cat crept in for its special new treat
Our dog smelled and sniffed at the tastiest meat
The chicken now long gone, in all shapes by me
Will feed pets tomorrow and us humans all three.

Donata Richards

WHAT YOU ARE TO ME

How can I describe what you are to me?
You are my first breath - and my last.
You are not just part of my world,
You have become my world,
I must stop, or you may disappear like wind into the unknown,
And to find someone like you would be an impossible dream,
Yet I must go on,
You are like the spring that blossoms at a touch,
You are like the summer, warm, yet becomes refreshed like the
                                                                  morning dew,
You are like the autumn, full in richness of a golden glory.
You are like winter, sparkling like the snow,
The cold outside, the warmest glow inside.
Now - I must really stop,
Or I may awaken one morning and find you gone.

Margaret Waudby

CHRISTMAS IN THE VILLAGE

One's been also a happy time,
In the village of the west,
Everybody tries to enjoy
And tries doing of their best.
What a reason you may ask,
Was a happy village so.
Or accomplish any task,
Or somebody somewhere go.
Reason was a simple one,
If one wonders what was that,
It comes at Christmas time.
Time enjoyment, conquest dead,
On the outside a white coat
Covers roads and all the land,
Bringing much disliked cold,
Which limited time to spend.
But when the end of December
Comes to our living gate,
Everyone would be a spender
And happiness must be paid.
In windows, Christmas tree
Show its beauty, colours light,
Which looking like a dream
In the middle village night.
So enjoy the village now
In these days, white like snow,
Days and nights of Christmas time
And happiness should still grow.

Kevin Kondol

HOUSEWIFE'S REVENGE

Cooking and cleaning, hoovering away,
Washing, ironing, busy all day!
No time for myself, no time to relax,
I'd love a soothing facial, maybe a leg wax,
My nails are broken, the varnish all chipped,
Hands sore and chapped, so are my lips!
'Oh, blow the housework, it's making me feel ill,
I'm off to the beauty parlour, send my husband the bill!'

Lesley Paul

THE CAT

A ball of fur! A tiresome lump.
My word, that cat gives me the hump.
Curled up on the hearthrug snug,
The handle missing from my best jug.
Up he jumps and out again,
Splashing about in mud and rain,
Jumps up the doors with his dirty paws,
Then skates back in over all the floors.

But me, I do not mind at all.
I love that great big furry ball.
He looks at me with pleading eyes,
As if to say 'I don't tell lies'
Opens his mouth with a great big yawn,
And then looks out upon the lawn,
Gone again, upon my word
He nearly had that little bird!

Now who says cats don't really know,
I open my mouth and I say, *'No!'*
He stops in his tracks as if to say,
I've heard that somewhere before today.'
Still motionless watching his 'might have been prey'
He rolls himself over and starts to play.

May Elliston

OUR SCHOOL

Look out the windows, and you can see
Where once a farmyard, used to be,
With cows, chickens and a bull,
Life was happy, never dull,
With a farmer, wife and dogs,
And a real fire, burning logs.
To the animals, he would call,
Now it's school,
It's Broadstone Hall!

D M Higgins

MY BELOVED

Where is my love?
Where can he be?
So far and distant,
Away from me!

A touch and a smile,
A long loving kiss;
His look of emotion,
I truly do miss.

Where is the music
That sang in my heart?
To comfort and guide me,
While we are apart.

Will he return?
Will love shine through?
To wonder and dream,
A life anew.

Anon

THINK OF ME

At the break of day as the sun starts to rise,
You can hear the birds singing as they take to the skies,
Then just for a moment think of me,
And I'll touch your heart, just fleetingly.
When you walk through a wood, look up to the trees,
And see their leaves rustling in a gentle breeze,
Then just for a moment think of me,
And I'll touch your heart, just fleetingly.
When you're watching the rain fall with its rhythmic sound,
As its dancing droplets hit the ground,
Then just for a moment think of me,
And I'll touch your heart, just fleetingly.
At the end of the day as you start to unwind,
All manner of thoughts go through your mind,
Then just for a moment think of me,
And I'll touch your heart, just fleetingly.
When the sky grows dark and day becomes night,
Look up at the stars there shining bright,
Then just for a moment think of me,
And I'll touch your heart, just fleetingly.
As you lie in bed, thoughts running deep,
Just before you fall asleep,
Then just for a moment think of me,
And I'll touch your heart, just fleetingly.

Pam Burley

ENGLAND 2004

With such skill from David Beckham,
The pushing power of Paul Scholes,
The talent of Owen and Rooney,
Will come good to score plenty of goals.
Nor forgetting the class of Frank Lampard,
Then there's Gerrard, such drive in his pass,
Sol Campbell, solid and strong in defence
Alongside Ashley Cole, my what class!
Garry Neville, a consistent defender,
John Terry shows plenty of flair,
David James, England's fine keeper -
Would be missed if he weren't there.
If needed, we have Emile Heskey,
Wayne Bridge and Darius Vassell,
Glen Johnson, Matthew Upson,
These talented players play well.
Paul Robinson, Chris Kirkland,
If needed could keep our goal,
Gareth Southgate, Kieron Dyer,
Not forgetting our Joe Cole,
Midfielders we have plenty
Should injuries cause a rut,
There's Hargreaves, Parker and Beatie
And the tenacious Nicky Butt,
Sven, the head coach for England
Has worked hard and brought our team up
So come on, lads, do the business,
Bring it home, 'yes' the Euro Cup!

Pamela Rossiter

WHERE LOVE SO TAINTED DWELLS

In a dream she knew my woe, my place of rest, of lily-white,
It's there we sleep, beyond the below, perhaps May, perhaps night.
This garden breathes no coloured air, it breeds unbridled passion,
Free to form a touch so rare, no more her love to ration.

Oh love of kin - for life with her, this the choice the learned have taught,
Not even the bravest of men to dare, 'Look at the shame your want has brought!'
In their ranks like soldiers drawn, they fought the father's eye,
Their hearts all scourged and tipped and torn, for love in life they strove to die.

Then lambent grew my earthly light, oh love for me would change their mind,
Had a tarnished soul not been forced to flight, we would have not reason for each line.
Amid the nonchalant solemn half-shadow, on t'ward a sense of someone near,
Led dangerously swift to a twilight meadow, through the crimson to an open clear.

Indeed she'd said it was our dream, her soul so flagrant on a scented zephyr,
I stared beyond a blue-green stream, beneath the willow I saw her.
Frosted moonlight kissed her nape, knelt low and difficult she moved,
A glinted tear so stained her face 'gainst the bark she traced our groove.

No sooner thought than had arrived, her touch in mine was then,
To lay there hence a kiss deprived, no trophy won for other men.
'Side the lakes of melting snows, no thought no more for given time,
Locked now close in deep repose,
Oh wantonness of heart sublime.

Ryan Kelly

THE LOVEBIRDS

Lovebirds are a bird to behold
Their faces red but not from the cold
They sing and chatter like lovers do
To show their love for me and you
They fill your home with screams and shout
To let you know their seed's run out
Then sit and snuggle up together
With love in their eyes that will last forever.

R Thompson

WHY?

My body lies peaceful, I look sound in slumber -
Why I have to wake, sometimes I wonder.
Slowly it starts . . . I shiver and shake
I know that soon I will wake.
For most people a new day is dawning
But for me - my eyes water and I just can't stop yawning.
This life is so hard, I wish I could die.
Most people say, 'Oh she just wants to get high!'
They don't understand - I so want to be free
From this dark cloud above that is following me.
They think that I do just to feel that I'm f****d
But that feeling goes the minute you're hooked.
Every day I wake up the same
And yeh! I know I've only myself to blame
But knowing that doesn't take it away
Still the hurting gets stronger day after day
And the more gear you need to make you feel well
Sometimes it feels like you're sentenced to Hell.
If I could just turn around and say - 'That's it - no more'
I tell you I'd have done it a long time before.
It just hurts me so much when you're without.
'Help me please, God' - I just want to shout
But no one can hear my cries so deep down
And I continue to wear my smile like a clown.
Hiding my shame and my hurt far inside
And hiding away all the tears that I've cried.
Pretending I'm fine and oh, so on top
And praying, 'Let *this* be the day I can *stop!*'

Becky Joyce

BECAUSE I LOVE YOU

Our love is special, I know it must be true,
Because I've never loved any man as much as I love you.
It isn't what you say and it isn't what you do.
It's the way you make me feel when I'm alone with you.

I've loved you from the beginning, I will love you to the end.
You have become such a part of my life that you're now my
                                                  closest friend.
'Friend', I use it loosely, because you're more than that to me.
One day I hope we will be more than friends but 'what will be will be'.

In my heart there's a special place that I've reserved for you.
No one can take this place, because it's special through and through.
It's my way of telling you that I really love and care,
And will always want to hold you close, when things seem so unfair.

To say 'I love you very much' is just a simple jest.
To say I love you more than that is because you are the best.
I would always love and care for you if you would only let me try.
There isn't anything I wouldn't do, and there's no need to ask why,

Because I love you.

Lynda Carol Beardmore

DEVIL'S DUST

You sold your soul to the Devil's dust
As you couldn't resist its seducing lust
It takes all your morals, you lie and you steal
Cheat on your friends, to secure the next deal
Think of your family, your children too
Would you like for them, what happened to you?
It shows no compassion for race or for creed
Spends all your money, for the habit you feed
Into your veins and into your blood
Gives your weak heart a terrible thud
Do you feel happy? Do you feel sad
Indulging your soul in this selfish fad?
Once you were so proud and true
Until that nasty evil came over you
Things they will go from bad to worse
All because of this terrible curse
You can rely on me when you die
As I've always been that kind of guy
You bore me a child, gave me great hope
But you chose to ignore us for that evil dope
You knew that we loved you, you knew that we cared
But it wasn't enough for your life to be spared
It's all over now, you'll never return
We're feeling so sad that you have to burn
We'll scatter your ashes, stand there and weep
And hope that you're watching, for memories to keep
One thing's for certain, I know it's true
We'll never stop showing our love for you
We've all got the heartache, we've all got the tears
But no one can take our happy years.

Steven Wilson

THERE'S A LOVE

There's a love for Mother Nature, the birds, the trees, the flowers;
There's a love for brilliant sunshine and also April showers.

There's a love for little children, our families and our friends;
It's such a wonderful feeling you never want to end.

There's a love for having freedom, from wars, and toil and strife;
There's a love for the Creator who guides us through our life.

But most of all, there is a love, which nothing can compare;
And that's for someone of your own, to cherish and to care.

It fills your very being, from each and every part,
Gives you cause for living and happiness in your heart.

Beth

I Won't Believe

How do we manage to get so caught up in the day, that we let all that is beauty slip by?
How in such insignificance do we find ourselves involved without a try?

It's extraordinary the wonders that go unnoticed,
as we traipse through each working day.
No pause for the amazement of happenings around us
as we sludge on our uneventful way.

It can't be what life's about, I won't believe it's what it's all for,
I'll just stop, stand still, take it all in as you pathetically carry on as before.

I won't become part of the rat race, what are you all out to prove?
Living to work, what is this about? I can't see I'll ever approve.

Do you ever do nothing, soak it all in, sit in silence, hear the birds sing?
Escape in awe of the mountains, watch the black sea at night?
Just take time with people, your family and friends, have you ever really listened to their plight?

I won't accept it, marching on in defiance; I'll rave on proving how you should care.
Thirty years slip by in the blink of an eye, while your life went from armchair, to office, to armchair.

T Milner

AN ETERNAL RELATIONSHIP

People often say
That nothing lasts forever
But what if every night you pray
'God in Heaven
Please make this last
Put my mistakes, errors and sins in the past
Through trials and tribulations
We'll get through them together

I need you now
More than ever
As the daily anxieties eat away at my mind
You always seem to make them go
Make me relax, unwind, take things slow
If you're not guiding me in prayer
You're always with me in spirit
I can always put my trust in you
As I acknowledge your works
Magnificent, inspiring and beautiful too

Since the day I became yours
You have become my best friend
I don't think anyone else could love me more
As long as I stay
True, joyful, fearful, helpful and faithful
I know you will never leave me
But always be
A truly good friend
Who sees beyond my outward appearance
Instead you see my heart, mind and true personality
I could, no, I will
Be with you eternally.'

Marco Nigro

BABYSITTING BLUES

I'm just doing my knitting while I'm babysitting
there must be more to life than this.
I should be out dancing and maybe romancing
and having my very first kiss.
Instead I sit with my wool, like a real stupid fool
for a couple of quid a night.
Listening for Amanda demanding her panda
something isn't quite right.
Why should my sister be out with her mister
and probably having a ball,
While I sit here scheming, thinking and dreaming
of nothing very much at all!

Kathy Duncan

EVE OF LOVE

New Year's Eve and the clock strikes twelve,

My heart, the life-giver, pumps the blood around my body,

I'm feeling the closeness, the warmth and kisses from my love,

Passion starts to burn inside as the explosions of colour open above my head.

Martin Bevan

Mongrels

Mongrels, that's what we are!
God created two people for one world
They cohabited in the Garden of Eden
And Cain and Abel came along
How dare you say we are not one
And one for all?

Mongrels, that's what we are!
Some went to faraway lands
To hide the grey area that nature brings
Mongrels start changing like a rainbow in the sky
Some change by the shining sun
While some change by the winter breeze.

Mongrels, that's what we are!
The water we drank, the air we breathed
The food we ate, the sun we tanned in
Are the reasons for our changes
From the land in the Garden of Eden.

Mongrels, that's what we are!
Dark eyes, slitty eyes, blue eyes, brown eyes
Curly hair, straight hair, short hair, long hair
Black, brown, white and pink
How did all these colours come along
Just like the rainbow in the sky?

Mongrels, mongrels, that's what we are!
Kings, queens, black and white
Peasants, noble, humble and wise
We are all mongrels, for we are not what we were at first
God made us in His own image
Now we have all sorts in this land
'Mongrels, mongrels, mongrels, forever mongrels'.

Some said we have third and first world
Now where is the second I'd like to know
Some brought wars and scars to this land
Some brought tears and fears in our hearts
Mongrels, mongrels, that's what we are!

May peace and love be the epitome of our dreams
And accept that we are mongrels hence
We should live in peace and harmony.

D Mullings-Powell

RITE OF PASSAGE

And they carry you in
draped
with the Union Jack
prepared
for a Viking's burial.

But there you stand,
curling a lock of hair
round a finger,
just like you always did
when lost for words.

Was it the swiftness
of your demise
that confused you,
or the sound
of your favourite song
Sailing
that holds you captive?

Music drowns
the sound of grief
when I lift my head
you're gone . . .

Fay Smith

So Tired

It is five past nine
I am tired
Bed is my domain

I'm worried
How can I sleep?
Nobody knows

I feel confused
Bottled up
Welling out of me from inside

Anger, aggression
Be false
For the time

Then -
Quiet
Calm

I float
My thoughts drift
I drift

It is five past ten
I am tired
Bed is my domain
Play the game again.

Sheena Harris

LOVE IS ETERNAL

Kisses, kisses, give me plenty
Whether I'm eighty or I'm twenty,
Give me cuddles, plenty more,
Whether for afters or before.

Words of love, words of honey,
Will make every day look sunny.
Tender touching, perfumed cheek,
And no winter will seem bleak.

Be most caring, be most gentle,
Love is heartfelt, not just mental,
Let us hug and let's coo on,
Today is here, tomorrow gone.

Let's be playful, let us pat,
What is better than all that?
Giving, taking, arm in arm,
Is our token good luck charm.

Let affection never grow cold,
We'll feel sprightly though we're old,
Youth's a state of mind and loin,
Come, my dearest, let us join.

Without love, life's so dreary,
Mortal struggling makes one weary,
But with loving one finds zest,
Dances, feasting, with the best.

Bliss is love that's well embedded,
Many suffer badly wedded,
But with you I just want more,
Let me love you to the core.

Emmanuel Petrakis

ROUNDABOUT OF LIFE

Gran rocks in her rocking chair,
Sunlight 'dances' on white hair
As a child, she listened to you
Special 'things' she did for you
Shared with her, soon were shed
All the worries in your head
Years have flown, quickly too
What happened to 'the little you'?
Roles reverse, wait and see
Give back all, love's not free!
It's your turn to give back all
As Gran did when you were small

Now Gran has worries in her head,
But told to you, soon are 'shed'
As off she goes to her warm bed
With these worries off her chest
Like you once, she now can rest
Years go by and we find out
Life is like a roundabout
Now that Gran is eighty-two
Give back the love, she gave to you.

Gran rocks in her rocking chair
Sunlight dances on white hair
Rounds of love, care and strife
On the 'roundabout of life'
All to old age are bound
As the years come around
The 'roundabout' of destiny's found.

Sheila Walters

MY GRANDMA

Never moans or groans
Never shouts or wears a frown
Always a kindly face
And will always take me any place,

To feed the ducks by the lake
Or lets me help to bake a cake.
Takes me shopping, or to the swings,
Has good ideas to do new things.

These gifts she gives - she has in store
Because she's done them once before.
For like my mum she understands
She's just a bit wiser -
That's why she's Grand.

Gill Green

THE DAYS OF THE WEST ARE DEAD

The wheels of the wagons are broken,
There's weeds 'round the ranch house door.
All the ponies are dead and gone,
We ain't gonna ride no more.
The bunkhouse is fallin' down,
Like the fences out on the spread.
No more campfires burnin'.
The days of the west are dead.

There's nothing left for us to do,
Now it's all folklore.
Our lives are shattered, friends are scattered
Just like in the Civil War.
All around you see ghost towns, no streets left, I'm afraid,
It really breaks my heart but the days of the west are dead.

There's nothing but dust and piles of rust,
Where the railroads used to be.
The railroad station, like the Indian nation,
We never more will see.
The rivers they have all dried up,
Now full of tumbleweed.
Nowadays it's an automobile, instead of your trusty steed.

No more gamblin', no more drinkin',
The saloons, they have all gone.
The old dog's lying there so sad,
'Cause he's been left there all alone.
The ranch is non-existent, just barren waste instead.
I feel distraught at the very thought
But the days of the west are dead.

Edward Mathieson

Busy Hands

Her hands were strong not pretty
The fingers long, were knuckled.
Nails were short and healthily pink
But oh! How very busy.

Those hands were restlessly working
All day at something new.
The garden to weed, fresh shrubs to display
By hands that were capably busy.

And yet what delicate patterns
Grew from soft wools and silks,
Woven and fused with the passionate touch
Of those hands so endlessly busy.

The tempting smells from the kitchen,
The dishes and trays of bakes,
Drew all like a magnet towards the display
By the working hands so busy.

Yet pause and consider the pain,
The sorrow of life's passing tide,
How a brow could be soothed with the delicate touch
From the hands that were always busy.

No polish or length of nail
But a ring of devotion and love,
Promised and worn on the finger of life,
On those hands that were so busy.

Pauline Bunkin

FULL CIRCLE

I came into this world with fine silky hair on my head
Not moving very much, just lying cosy in my bed

I had no teeth to chew with, no T-bone stake for me
All I got was Mother's milk 'cause that we got for free

I liked my milk, I enjoyed my milk, I had no need to quibble
I just wish my mum wouldn't fill me up to the point where
                                                      I would dribble

While lying comfy in my bed, all warm, content and happy
Someone would come and pick me up cos me milk's ended
                                                      up in me nappy

Of course I was too small to walk, I couldn't even crawl
I just liked being held, being cuddled, being wrapped up in my shawl

It's a little like the one I have now lying round me from shoulder
                                                      to shoulder
For you see I have come full circle, I am now a lot, lot older

Once again I have no teeth of my own and milk I drink a lot
Once again I can't get myself to the loo, I have to use a pot

Once again my hair is fine and silky, here and there you can see
                                                      my head
And I seem to need a lot of rest, I spend far more time in bed

Someone has to help me dress, help me bath and brush my hair
For you see I have come full circle, back to needing full-time care.

Avril Brown

MY BLACK ROSE

In all this world you would never suppose
That you would ever see a black rose
There's red, white and pink ones too
They are everyday colours like me and you

To me they are nothing as you would see
There's only one colour that means something to me
You talk of beauty, God knows why
You've never seen it so why do you try?

To find that beauty, you'd never succeed
You'd travel the world, still never been seen
But I have found it so now I will tell
You will all be proud as I am as well

You all looked for beauty in flowers and pearls
But you made a mistake because it's a girl
This girl is so special I want you to see
There's no girl living could touch her for me

She's got dark skin and lovely black hair
She's the pride of my life and that's why I care
I will always love her but this you must know
Her name's Margaret Jackson and I love her so.

Roy Jackson

A Beautiful Mind
(A tribute to Mrs John Nash)

You are all my reason, you are my belief
The history high above me, the mystery that lies beneath.
You are all my logic, the truth in what I see
That takes you far away, Love, then brings you back to me

You are the equation to the problem that gives my thoughts
                                                     much needed rest
And when they bring out the worst in me
You bring back the best

You are my alpha and omega, my beginning and my end
Wife, companion, lover, helper, protector, friend,
Staunch and believing
When belief is hard to find
Kind heart, loving smile beats achieving
Beautiful heart, beautiful soul, beautiful mind.

S Beverly Ruff

Untitled

The thought came
Whilst lost
In reverie.
How much more
There must be,
Existing in this
World
That I will
Never hear.
Music that would
Touch my heart.
Words that
Would resound
With mine.
Am I creating
Theirs, or
Are they
Creating mine?
Across the
Universe a
Thought precedes
Reality.
Does their music
Prompt my
Flowing words,
Or mine
Create their
Song?
Vibrations from
An age
Gone by
Are suddenly
Reborn.

My thoughts
Too create
A ripple
In another
Space and
Time.

Fran Gardner

My Twilight World

Deep in the depths of my mind
Are caverns of a myriad kind
I must explore them to try to see
This other world which is inside me
To enter this place I then have to keep
A rendezvous when I am half asleep
Then I can travel deep down inside
And all at once it becomes alive
While in this strange and altered state
Am I dreaming or am I awake?
Through the haze now I can see
Shadowy figures close to me
They glimpse at me as they glide by
Like floating clouds in the sky
What is this inner world of mine
That seems so different in another time?
Only my mind knows what is there
And maybe one day its secret it will share
All the mysteries of the deep
In my twilight world when I am half asleep.

Robert Beach

I Wish

I wish that I could be free to swim the sea,
I wish that I could be someone else and not always me.
I wish that I could fly over this land,
I wish that I could win 100 grand.
With all that money I could move to a new place,
then no more wishing for some quiet space.
Just to be free would be the biggest prize yet,
but I've never been a person who likes to bet.
I wish I could run and jump up in the sky,
leave this place behind and not have to say goodbye.
Wishes only come true if you mean what you're wishing for,
my wishes have never come true in my life before.
Yet I mean every word that comes out of my mouth,
I wish I could get out of this godforsaken house!

Rachel Krastins (13)

Looking Back From Above

I closed my eyes to see that old mountaintop
Where once I would climb to sit upon a rock
When I looked to the valley below
Memories of old began to flow
To a time where everyone wore a smile
Cares of this world were not mine
When laughter was heard all around
What a beautiful feeling hearing that sound
When life was as carefree as a bird
Bad talk of anyone was never heard
We all lived together down in that valley
Neighbours them all were part of the family

Everyone was there to help each other
We could always rely on one another
Everyone seemed to understand
It was your duty to lend a neighbour a hand
The love in that valley no one could hide
It broke my heart, the day I left with the tide
To start a new life on a foreign shore
Like so many had done before
But now as my life nears its end
Dear Lord to that valley, my soul please send
That special place I was forced to depart
But I treasured forever, deep in my heart.

Michael Chambers

INTOXICATED DEMONS

The cold grey light of dawn
scatters shadows from the darkness in my mind
and brighter pictures dance around
like trapped sunlight in this empty bottle of mine
but every waking day remains the same
I slowly go from sane to insane
on this damp park bench where I drink away my pain
how times change, priorities rearrange
I'm cold and I'm old and I'm fading away
into another endless day.

And the voices inside my tortured mind
chase away the lonely hours
and all that time devours,
as I search the broken back streets for a sign
but I can't find my past, the sunlight doesn't last
my fading memory of my family is like cracked glass
broken with a celestial arrow from a dying rainbow
as thoughts of Heaven's peace come and go
will I find the strength tomorrow to wake at all?
Why can't the freezing rain release the pain my thoughts contain?
But sad images are felt once the cards get dealt
and my intoxicated demons, will forever cage my freedom
but if I take the endless sleep
this poem carved into an old damp bench
is yours to keep.

Mathew Cullum

The Gardening Club

The gardening club was held one night.
Two pots you had to bring.
The subject that was chosen
Was planting bulbs for spring.

We all sat on the platform steps
To get a better view
As the expert shared his knowledge
And showed us what to do.

When the bulbs had all been planted
To each one's satisfaction,
Grandad scooped a massive load
And hurried into action.

Filling up his planted pots
Laying fibre with haste
Building layers of discarded bulbs
He couldn't bear to waste.

Grandad took the bulbs back home
But to replant them he forgot
And in the spring the bulbs did shoot
There really was a lot.

Daffodils, hyacinths,
Each of different hue.
All mixed up with tulips
Stuck together like glue.

The planting was disastrous
He's given up the club
He's had enough of blooming bulbs
And now goes down the pub.

Edith Mary Wilson

ALTARS

I brought to you, tall daffodils in bowls,
Their bowed, curved heads still brushed and bright with dew;
Beeswaxed dressers caught and held the sun's scrolls;
Through opened windows, scented breezes blew.
I gave these tokens of your final spring
As keepsakes of the life you'd leave behind:
The pain; delight; words you'd no longer sing;
Cow-parsleyed lanes our steps would no more wind.
Like some bridal posy of violets,
You'd take our vows to altars of the soil,
Cradling our marriage at its sunset:
A restless sea veined and stilled by love's oil.
Through bluebell waves in woods, I glimpsed your ghost:
Sensing that beauty shared is never lost.

James Knox Whittet

DRAGON TALES - TIMOTHY THOMAS

Timothy Thomas wished he could
    Play with the children in the wood.
Although he was huge, he was gentle and kind
    When children climbed over him, he didn't mind.
He'd patiently sit while they tumbled and slid
    Off his back or his tail and whatever they did
He would happily join them in games that they played
    Until, one tragic day, a small toddler strayed.
They all hunted and searched . . . but they couldn't discover
    Where the toddler hid, where he'd gone undercover
Till someone screamed . . . ! They had found him . . . quite flat . . .
    Beneath some tall grass, just where Timothy sat.
Poor Timothy cried . . . but it did him no good.
    The children, forbidden to go into the wood
Would stand in the sunshine, pressed close to the wire
    And call out and wave . . . and as sadly, retire . . .
Timothy just couldn't play in the sun . . . !
    And so . . . gone forever . . . his playmates, his fun.
And he sighed . . . oh so sadly . . . and wished that he could
    Play with the children, in the wood . . .

Olive R Thomson

TROUBLED MIND

Troubled mind, please be kind
Don't let's throw it all away on this
Troubled mind, please be kind
We both deserve much more than this.

You and me cannot see what hurt we cause,
But we can change
And we will set your demons free
Then you'll see how happy you can be.

Lift the shades from your eyes,
There's no one really to despise
Learn to give and you will live
Don't forget how to forgive
Stay with me
Eventually
You will be free

Your torture's in your mind
Leave it behind
It's not your friend
It may be your end
No one needs to see
How bad bad can be
Don't fight yourself
Just let it be.

Alexander Campbell

CJ

CJ, today, tomorrow and every day
Let the people of this nation
Put their hand on their hearts and say
'We did you no wrong.'
When liars lied
To save our national hide
You took the flack
Came back from the abyss
And showed us the way
We saw a nation rise from its knees
And stand tall
Alongside others we looked up to in awe
Your outward look
And inward tuck
Saw the nation's coffers fill
And cranes jostle for supremacy
Over a Dublin skyline
Like the good salesman
You sold your product well
You plucked your words with precision
And executed them with eloquence
Showed cead mile failte
To the stranger in your own home
Partied until the dawn
Sneaked in under Portmarnock
Time now for your morning ride out
On Malahide's golden sand
And later on your skippered your yacht
Into the sunset with a smile
Upon your face
Yet you showed feet of clay
When you strayed from a purple path
Where few can take
A life-long walk

Patriot, statesman uncrowned high-king
Or home-grown country squire
Make your mind up time
And now you follow
The path of the wild geese
South to a Bourgeois Land
Not a door slammed fast to ignominy
CJ today, tomorrow and every day
A memory to never fade away

James Gallagher

RAINDROP

A single raindrop falls from somewhere way up high
I feel its icy touch as rain clouds fill the sky
My clothes and my heart start to dampen and from misty glasses
                                                                                                        I stare
The wind whips across my face and little streams of water run
                                                                                                       from my hair.

The wind blows, the sea rises and crashes against the pier
Seagulls screech, take flight and wheel away in fear
The spray wets the prom, children blown along as if on skis
The coastguard returning to port cutting through raging seas

Suddenly there's a chink in the sky, sunlight bursts through a
                                                                                             beacon of light
The horizon is an array of shining colours brighter than firework night
The clouds now disperse, waves flatten to a calm
I open my hand, the last raindrop wet on my palm.

Alan Brafield

SUBMISSIONS INVITED
SOMETHING FOR EVERYONE

OVER £10,000 POETRY PRIZES TO BE WON!

POETRY NOW 2004 - Any subject, any style, any time.

WOMENSWORDS 2004 - Strictly women, have your say the female way!

STRONGWORDS 2004 - Warning! Opinionated and have strong views. (Not for the faint-hearted)

All poems no longer than 30 lines.
Always welcome! No fee!
Cash Prizes to be won!

Mark your envelope (eg *Poetry Now*) **2004**
Send to:
Forward Press Ltd
Remus House, Coltsfoot Drive,
Peterborough, PE2 9JX
(01733) 898101

If you would like to order further copies of this book or any of our other titles, please give us a call or log onto our website at
www.forwardpress.co.uk